The Idanha

Courtesy Garret Photography

The Idanha

The Idanha

Guests and Ghosts of An Historic Idaho Inn

By
Dick d'Easum

CAXTON PRESS
Caldwell, Idaho
2001

First printing, 1984
Second printing, January, 2001

Library of Congress Cataloging in Publication Data

D'Easum, Dick.
The Idanha : guests and ghosts of an historic Idaho inn.

1. Idanha (Hotel : Boise, Idaho) I. Title.
TX941.I3D4 1983 647'.947962801 83-7564

ISBN 0-87004-414-1

Printed and bound in the United States of America
CAXTON PRESS
Caldwell, Idaho 83605
166747

Dedication

For Kathleen
Who gave sisterly approval to
my first professional haircut
at the Idanha

Acknowledgements

This story of a landmark was intended to be a brief account of a picturesque old hotel. The more research progressed, the larger became the chest of treasures sparkling in the long career of an inn built to maintain traditions of the Overland House.

The history proved to be so full of lively events and people it could not be compressed into a short article. The Idanha is a focal point in Idaho history. Its record is full of guests and ghosts, royalty and rogues, honeymoons and homicides. Events at the Idanha through more than eighty years are closely linked to development of Boise and the state.

I appreciate the assistance of the Idaho Historical Society in providing periodicals and pictures. Notes and suggestions from Arthur Hart, director, have been particularly useful. Many members of the staff gave patient help. Without the cooperation and information of Mrs. Ansgar Johnson and Mrs. Alice Tetrick Bellomo, each a former proprietor of the Idanha, the book could not have been written. Essential data was also supplied by Jess Jennison, a former manager. Senator Woody Nelson, prime minister of public relations, has contributed priceless bits of hotel lore. To all of them I am thankful.

Dick d'Easum

Introduction

Idanha may be an Indian word meaning "healing waters." It way be an English word meaning "bubbling waters." Whatever its origin in fancy or fact, the word has meant to Boise and a wide section of the Pacific Northwest a turreted hotel, steeped in history, crammed with memories of famous and notorious people, a proud survivor among traditional inns wiped out by the motel flood.

The Idanha was opened to the public with drums and flourishes in 1901 and is still accommodating guests in most of the 140 rooms on its six floors that drew "ohs" and "ahs" of appreciation when it plumped its first pillow and poured its first champagne. Actually, the Idanha at Tenth and Main streets is the second hotel of that name in Idaho. The original was at Soda Springs. It was built in 1887 by the Natural Mineral Water Company of Ogden, Utah, and operated, in part, as a dining station for the Union Pacific Railroad. Like its Boise namesake, the Soda Springs Idanha was distinguished by turrets and European furnishings with classical flavor. Mineral water, which still gushes from several springs at Soda, was dispensed liberally. It was touted as good for many ailments and was very good indeed for the bank accounts of people who bottled and sold it. The healing water was served with meals and made available in pitchers for overnight guests. The hotel building was remodeled into apartments many years before it was destroyed by fire in 1921.

Whether the proprietors of the Boise Idanha picked up the name from Soda Springs is not known. Minutes of corporation meetings reveal nothing. There is logical speculation, however, that the men who planned the Boise venture were aware of the Idaho ancestor and probably of some other Idanhas scattered around the United States.

One thing is common among all the Idanhas. The spelling is dealer's choice. Sometimes it is Idan-Ha. Sometimes it is I-Dan-Ha. Occasionally it comes up Ida-Na-Ha. A few cutesy advertisements start the name with a picture of an eyeball and follow it with "Dan" and "Ha," with or without hyphens.

How the prime movers in the Idanha of Boise chose the name is of academic interest compared with the product they created. The Idanha Hotel Company was organized by Thomas McMillan, John McMillan, John W. Cage, Robert Aikman, and James B. Morrow. One of the important reasons they went into the hotel business was that the Overland, long a famous stopping place, was about to give up the ghost. Pioneers who revered the Overland saw the need for a hotel that would meet the requirements of Boise's ten thousand residents and the growing population of Idaho. All the incorporators were of the pioneer generation, although they did not qualify with the elite of the 1860s. All except Cage were livestock growers. Cage had been a manager of the Overland. That was just what the board wanted; the company made him manager.

The formal opening on January 3, 1901, followed a private party for selected guests. None of the people who swarmed through the lobby and the rooms, and certainly not manager Cage, could have imagined what dramas and what a cast would make the Idanha a caldron of triumph, amazement, and tragedy. Regardless of the true meaning of Idanha, the hotel has never been a placid pool. Hot or healing, perhaps, but never stagnant.

For instance, at the Idanha:

Gov. Frank Steunenberg, a frequent guest, nearly lost his life to a Harry Orchard bomb. The assassin, who later did kill the former governor in Caldwell, disconnected his Idanha bomb for fear it would harm a chambermaid.

Walter Johnson, the Weiser kid, limbered his arm in a hall while waiting for rain to stop. His catcher fetched a thundermug for home plate. Tradition says Johnson shattered the porcelain with a low curve.

William Jennings Bryan, perennial candidate for president, ordered a tub of ice on a hot day after a Boise speech. A girl slipped into the presence of the Great Commoner ahead of the bellboy. All three were embarrassed, particularly Bryan, who was standing in front of an electric fan in his shorts.

Sally Rand slept there — probably on a feather fed.

A son of Tommy Manville took a job as elevator operator while his mother was getting a quickie Idaho divorce.

The Royal Canadian Mounted Police caught its man at the Idanha. He was accused of a financial sting. Oops! Wrong man. The generally reliable mounties added red faces to their red jackets.

An outraged husband shot the lover of his wife four times when he caught them in a compromising situation. The scandal took top billing from the Haywood-Orchard court proceedings.

Ethel Barrymore and maid occupied the choice suite when she attended the Haywood trial. Her appearance in court with Gifford Pinchot, head of the Forest Service, unjointed Clarence Darrow's nose. Darrow, the famous defense attorney, frequented the lobby, talking with other attorneys and the press.

William E. Borah delivered his vindication speech from the Main Street balcony after he was acquitted of juggling timber claims.

A fan, belly, or strip dancer at a Boise nightclub forgot to tell a boyfriend about her roommate. When he opened her door late one night, he and about half the hotel's customers ran screaming into the street as an eight-foot python slithered down the corridor.

James Corbett, heavyweight champion who knocked out John L. Sullivan, skipped rope in the hall. He was on a speaking tour advocating clean habits and regular exercise.

The bride of one of Boise's richest Chinese merchants stayed at the Idanha just before her wedding, which was one of Boise's most elaborate. In earlier years the Idanha, in common with most hotels of the region, did not employ Chinese, let alone accept them as guests.

A bust of Idanha (or Hiawatha or Pocahontas) ornamented the lobby for many years. Its eyes were rigged with red lights to glow when the bust was moved. Thieves cut the apparatus and made off with the bust. It has not been recovered.

Charles Grout, manager from 1908 to 1913, had been a dining car manager for the Oregon Short Line. He enjoyed food so much that one of the first airplanes to visit Boise could not take him as a passenger. It could not get his poundage off the ground.

Pablo Casals bowed his cello in an Idanha room while practicing for a concert at the Pinney.

C. B. Wilson, legislator from Caribou County, pattered across the lobby in his stocking feet when he arrived past midnight, for fear his shoe treads might wake people.

Polly Bemis, the noted Chinese bride from Warren, had her first elevator ride, first motion picture, and first streetcar ride while a guest at the Idanha.

A ghost wanders one floor, opening locked doors, turning on showers and moaning down the elevator shaft.

George Cordes, long-time cafe manager, had been a marathon runner in his native Greece. He sponsored athletic teams in Boise and served thousands of free dinners to unfortunates at Christmas and Thanksgiving.

A man from Chicago stopped for a cup of coffee and a doughnut during the time gangsters were in flower. He ate his snack while his taxi clicked to $135 and the driver napped. The fare said he was headed for someplace in Oregon — most anywhere — because he thought it wise to come west in a hurry. The case remains a mystery.

Ted Lewis twirled his cane, tipped his top hat, and sang "Is everybody happy?" from the top of the counter in the cafe.

Hogan the Stiff, one of Boise's most imaginative drunks, collected a brick from behind the Idanha and hurled it through the window of a nearby music store. The brick disembowled a phonograph Hogan said was talking naughty to him with its horrible sounds. What he would have thought of the Beatles and the Splitting Headaches can be guessed. For his appreciation of better music Hogan did ten days. He told the court he was not sorry.

A recent public relations representative of the Idanha, a character with P. T. Barnum genes, got ten votes for president in 1980. He did not concede to Ronald Reagan until all polls closed.

With personages and activities like these as common fare it is no wonder that Mrs. Roxie Johnson, daughter of founder Tom McMillan and herself hotel manager for several years, has said that the Idanha had no competition. "There have been other hotels," she said. "They were contemporaries, not rivals. We sent them customers now and then because we didn't have room."

The Idanha was built on a corner in Boise's business district that had been the site of the Presbyterian church. The lot was next to property owned by Peter Sonna, prominent community builder for many years. The McMillans, Scotch Presbyterians, worked out a deal favorable to the church, which had already build a new house of worship away from the hustle and bustle, and in return gave the hotel company the land it wanted near the center of expanding Boise.

The IDAN-HA

Obie Corder and family had a strong influence on the development of western Idaho. James O. Corder, proprietor of a trading post at what later became Mayfield, toned down the Indian uprising of 1878, thereby saving lives and property of settlers. He put out ranching roots. Through his family he was also the grandpa of the Idanha Hotel, a public oasis he never dreamed of at his travelers' roost on a branch of the Oregon Trail, where sagebrush was eight feet tall and Bannock braves whipped up war dances.

This was the connection with the Idanha:

A daughter of Corder and his wife, Anna Blaylock, was Roxie Corder. She married Thomas McMillan, a native of Scotland. McMillan and associates built and operated the Idanha for many years. Mrs. Roxie Johnson, a daughter of Tom McMillan and Roxie Corder, managed the hotel after her father died. Since the McMillan era the Idanha has had two corporate ownerships — a derivative of the Broadbent estate and, most recently, Idanha Properties, including White-Savage Associates.

With that as a link to the Idanha history it is appropriate to give more details of the Corder chronicle. As an Indiana farm boy of sixteen he put down his hoe and hired out with

James O. Corder, pioneer rancher and trader at Mayfield, was the patriarch of the family that built the Idanha.

a freight string heading for the gold of California. It was the spring of 1850, and the cream had been skimmed. Corder found slim pickings. After ups and downs — here a nugget, there a flop — he quit mining for the cattle business. Early in that work he tangled with Indians, an experience that influenced his career in Idaho. Main points of that adventure and other significant events are told in a manuscript by Irene Corder, another daughter. The title is "Mr. and Mrs. James Obidiah Corder: A Short History of their Pioneer Life in the West from 1833 to 1929."

The spelling of Obidiah varies. Some times it is Obediah. The biblical character for whom most "Obie" men are named is Obadiah. He is known in his short chapter for having a vision. Unlike many sires in the Old Testament he didn't begat much. However, Obidiah Corder did have vision for a land of happiness and enterprise in Idaho. He was strong for begatting, too. He begat eleven children.

"Father would often entertain us with Indian stories," the biography by Irene Corder says. "One was when he lived in Humboldt County, California. He and several men were driving cattle along the Pacific coast. The Indians went ahead of them and hid in the rocks, intending to kill them and take the cattle. There was a trail just below where the Indians hid and where the cattle had to be driven. They did not wish to go along the shore because the tide would come in before they could get through. They had to take their chances to either drown in the ocean or be killed by the Indians. They decided to take their chances against the Indians. They might kill a few while they were being shot at. There were several men with father, one of which was killed later by Indians near Salmon, Idaho by the name of Jim Hayden. He was always deathly afraid of Indians and said they would someday kill him.

"Father took the lead. He told his men: 'Now boys we must make a charge on our horses with our guns loaded and in our hands. If any Indian shows his head take good aim and make a good Indian of him and keep running.'

"When the Indians saw father they yelled: 'We will get

Obe this time.' He had had fights with them before and always told them he would not be killed by an Indian. They took aim but he was too quick for them and got his Indian. This time again they took aim and shot father's hat off and yelled that they had got him. But he shot and got another one. The third time they shot they killed his horse and he thought his time had come. But one of his men came to the rescue and said: 'Climb on behind me as quick as you can as it is getting pretty hot here.' They took off as fast as their horses could run. The Indians yelled: 'Obe, we will get you next time.' None of the men were killed. He did say it was the closest he ever came to being shot by Indians. He had friends among that tribe and knew when they plotted to kill him. So he was always on the lookout.

"Father had an Indian boy he raised from a child. He came to Idaho with him in 1864 and they built a cabin on Indian Creek. He and his partners brought their cattle from California to Idaho and sold them in Idaho City and Rocky Bar. The Indian boy was used to a warmer climate. He contracted pleurisy and died suddenly. Father was in Idaho City when the boy became sick but did not get back before he died. He kept asking for Mr. Obe and told my mother often as he helped her milk the cows, 'Mister Obe is a good man and thinks lots of you.'

"Mrs. Corder was Anna Graham Blaylock. She was born in Cedar Rapids, Iowa in 1847. She crossed the plains three times with her parents after the discovery of gold in California. Her father had come from Ohio to Iowa with his parents and filed on timberland for farming. Clearing the timber was difficult work. Her father developed bronchitis and was in poor health. He married when very young and got tired of farm life. He thought traveling in the out-of-doors would restore his health. He made four trips to California by wagon. He left his family with his parents the first trip. His wife taught school and had the oldest girl, Hannah, with her. Anna, who was too young for school, stayed with her grandparents. Her father went to California in 1850 and came back the next year. He liked the climate, the gold mining and blazing the trail so well he took his family West in 1852. It took from spring until fall to go from Keokuk, Iowa to Sacramento.

"There was evidence all along the trail where cattle, horses, dogs, and mules had died. Also there was bedding and furniture that had to be left behind to lighten loads. Anna saw a beautiful doll by the roadside but her father would not let her pick it up because they could not carry extras. She didn't think a doll would make any difference. She never forgot that doll.

"On their first trip after reaching California, her father sold his wagons and mules and they returned by ship through Panama. . . . On their second trip her father persuaded his parents and a brother and his family to also come west. They settled in Hangtown (near Placerville). They gave it that name because there was so much robbing and killing of miners for gold dust. There were no lawmen, so the miners got together, caught the guilty parties and hung them to the nearest tree. When we visited there in 1927 we saw a big replica of a bull called the 'Hangtown bull.'

"Mrs. Corder and her older sister, Hannah, would carry lunches to miners and while they were eating they would loan their gold pans to the girls and tell them to pan gold for themselves. The girls accumulated several nuggets this way. When they returned to Iowa each bought a sidesaddle with a red plush seat. Her father and his parents grew tired of the west and returned to Iowa to try farming again. But three cents a dozen for eggs and other farm prices in the same range were pretty low. So the fourth trip west was planned. This time they intended to go through Idaho and winter in Portland. That was the spring of 1862. They were fortunate on these trips and never had any trouble with the Indians. They traveled with several other wagons and at night would circle the wagons and rope the openings to make a corral for their cattle and horses. They always had two or three men on guard.

"The Indians would first try to steal the horses and then

kill the immigrants. But her father was never afraid. The only time Mrs. Corder was afraid was on the last trip. She was riding a fine bay horse and he could smell the Indians and carried on and snorted when Indians were close. She had ridden ahead of the wagons and as it was about camping time had stopped at a creek to let her horse eat. Suddenly he raised his head and snorted. There were two buck Indians coming in front of her. Her horse turned toward the wagons, running as fast as he could go, with the Indians right behind. Her horse outran them. When she got back to the wagons she turned her horse over to the men. She was so frightened she sat down and shook all over.

"The Indians came over and said, 'White man's squaw heap scared.' She thought if they had caught her they would have taken her captive. She was very careful not to get so far away from the wagons again and was sure the horse had saved her life.

"In the fall of that year they stopped at Indian Creek (now Mayfield) 24 miles from Boise. The owner had a fine garden and had talked to Mr. Blaylock at Camas Prairie and suggested they stop there and take all the vegetables they could eat. It was a desolate-looking place and the women did not want to stop. Her father told Anna to get out and look at the notice the owner had left to see if it was the right place. It was. She thought she would tell him 'no,' but knew better than to tell her parents a falsehood. Her father said they would camp there for the night. They picked the first fresh vegetables they had eaten since Iowa and they were a treat.

"The owner persuaded them to winter there. So they built a log cabin with a fireplace, expecting to go on to Oregon in the spring. Instead, Anna lived at that same place until 1904 when she and Mr. Corder sold their ranch to their oldest son, William Corder, and bought a home in Boise at 1120 Hays Street.

"After building the cabin, her parents decided they would build a travelers' house and serve meals to the public. They also set up the first stage station east of Boise.

They fed and cared for stage horses. The stage line always drove four horses and maintained a relay station every 16 to 24 miles. They served meals to stage drivers and passengers.

"That fall James O. Corder and his partners, Jim and Milt Kelly, and George Aden arrived from California with a herd of beef cattle. They also built a cabin on Indian Creek. Because they were from California Mr. Blaylock was interested in them and called them his California boys. They had crossed the plains in search for gold and had given that up for the cattle business. They sold most of their beef herd in Idaho City and Rocky Bar. They often ate their meals at the Blaylock home. Because young ladies were not plentiful they were most anxious to get acquainted with Miss Anna Blaylock.

"She was so bashful she would not let them see her and would never wait on tables while they were there. One morning during breakfast she told her mother she would go milk the cow while they were eating. So she put on her shaker bonnet and took off with the milk bucket. But Obe had told his partners he would not leave there that morning without speaking to Miss Blaylock. He saw her leave the house, hurried his breakfast and went to the corral where she was milking to catch his horse. He took his rope, caught his horse and rode close to the cow she was milking to see if she would stand up. She kept her head close to the cow's flank so he could not see her face and kept on milking. After he rode off, thinking he had failed in his mission, she stood up to see what sort of rider he was. He tipped his hat and said 'Goodbye Miss Blaylock.' She went to the house laughing about it, and told her mother that he was awfully smart. She said he was making fun of her because she was so bashful. They got acquainted right after that and were married March 20, 1865. He later bought the Indian Creek ranch from her father. Her folks bought a ranch on Bowns Creek and kept a stage station there. In addition to his interest in cattle and horses, Mr. Corder built a trading post. He raised many horses. They had wonderful grass range all year. In 1884 he sold many head for $45 but he had some horses that went for as much as $600 each.

"At his trading post he sold groceries, blankets of all colors, looking glasses, war paint, calico, ribbons, and beads for Indian moccasins. Indians always bought sugar and other groceries in small amounts. They were afraid if they bought more than they could figure themselves they might be cheated. Mr. Corder told them if they bought 100 pounds of sugar it would be cheaper. They wouldn't do it. The captains and other leaders of the Bannocks understood better and bought in quantities. They also brought all kinds of furs to trade, including beaver, mink, otter, wolf, and buffalo robes. Mr. Corder would take these furs he traded from the Indians and sell them in Boise to the Falk brothers.

"Corder had just bought a robe from a young Indian for $10. A few minutes later he sold it to a stage passenger for $20. Eastern men on the stage were always interested in hides, particularly buffalo robes. After the sale the Indian didn't look happy. He said to Corder: 'You gave me $10 for the robe and sold it for $20. You cheatem George.' Corder said: 'No cheat you. Robe only worth $10. Cheat white-man.' The Indian thought that was all right.

"He always had a way of making friends with the Indians. When the Bannock war broke out in 1878 these Indians came to buy paint and ribbons and groceries to go on the warpath as they were mad at the government. Many had hired out as scouts in the Nez Perce war. When they returned the government would not give them soldier's wages of $10 a month. They were paid off in old bacon and other inferior food. Mr. Corder went to Fort Boise to intercede for the Indians. But the government wouldn't listen.

"When war broke out on Camas Prairie the Indians told Mr. Corder they would not hurt him or his family and they could stay home. When they did come through they stole the neighbor's horses but none of his. After the war when the Bannocks were rounded up and put on the reservation they asked the agent to write Mr. Corder requesting his store bill. The amount was rather sizable. He trusted them through fall and winter. When spring came they would bring their furs to pay the bill. He relied on that. The amount he eventually received was more than the bill. They said that was the interest. This proved to him that the Indians were more honest than most whites.

"Mr. and Mrs. Corder had 11 children, all born on Indian Creek except the oldest son, William, who was born in Boise. Two of their children, Obie and Anna, were twins. They were a great curiosity to the Indians. When they came to the store they always wanted to see the twins. They called Anna 'Dirty Face' and Obie 'Clean Face.'

"There were many horse thieves in those early days along the Oregon Trail. They would drive off immigrant horses and hide them in the brush. The owners would usually hunt a few days and give up. One group camping at Mr. Blaylock's ranch lost horses to the thieves. He had heard a bunch of horses being driven by that night so he suggested to the travelers that they go up Indian Creek several miles and look in the brush. They found their horses tied there. He asked them not to mention that he had told them because he did not want the thieves to be his enemies.

"The same people made bogus gold dust and paid Mr. Blaylock with it. He took it to Boise where a merchant discovered it was bogus. He took the dust back and paid in cash for his groceries. Later the thieves returned to Mayfield and again offered to pay their bill in gold dust. He told them about taking the first batch to Boise where it was found worthless. They asked him to give back the old batch and they gave him real dust for it.

"Finally people got tired of the horse stealing and bogus gold. They decided to hang a few thieves, hopeful that this would put a stop to it. Some men from Boise stopped at Indian Creek and asked Mr. Corder to help in rounding up the outlaws who had a camp on Canyon Creek near Long Tom, about 16 miles from Indian Creek. Mr. Corder declined because they had never done him any harm even though they might be guilty. They caught and hanged two of the thieves. One was named Updike. This was the only hanging along Overland Road in those days. There were many fights with fists and guns at Indian Creek. Mrs. Corder was very brave. She always said she didn't want anybody killed at her place. When a quarrel started she told them that if they had any respect for a lady and children they would quit at once. And they would. They generally ended their quarrels.

"Mr. and Mrs. Corder lived on Indian Creek 40 years. They fed and gave shelter to many a hungry person. In 1865 Boise was a town of many tents but few houses. The Corder place was a stage stop known to everyone. The Corders had many real friends in Boise including the Falks, Coffins, Eastmans, Somes, Lemps, Cap Griffin, owner of the Overland Hotel; Bush, owner of the Central Hotel; and Mr. Mobley who called the square dances. There were also the Haileys, Lusks, Boomers, O. P. Johnson, the cattleman; Catlin, another stockman; Wm. Rice, the stage driver; Ridenbaughs, Wiels, and the Blacks of Black's Creek. Mr. Corder had a big orchard and a variety of fruit, especially his China peaches — three weighed two pounds. He also had lots of melons. (They often took trips to Rocky Bar and Atlanta to hunt and fish. Mary Black Ridenbaugh accompanied them on one of those vacations. The Corders also visited the Matt Grahams on summer excursions. Matt Graham was a mining man with properties in several places, including Silver Mountain in Boise County.)

"They moved to Boise in 1904 and bought a home at 1120 Hays Street. Mr. Corder died in 1907 and Mrs. Corder in 1929. She was survived by one son, Grover C. Corder, and six daughters: Mrs. A. W. Beck (Jenny), Irene, Mrs. George Breckenridge (Anna), Mrs. Thomas McMillan (Roxie), Mrs. Kenneth Compton (Ida), and Mrs. Eugene Walker (Lula). She was a member of the First Presbyterian Church in Boise for 33 years."

The IDAN-HA

John and Thomas McMillan, prime movers in starting the Idanha Hotel, arrived at Mayfield soon after the most exciting times at Corder's station. The brothers were born in Scotland. John, the elder, went to the ranch in 1881. He got the job of postmaster and had the name changed to Mayfield for his old home in Scotland. Thomas followed in 1886. He had been a bank clerk in Glasgow. He herded sheep in Wyoming before coming farther west. He established a sheep outfit at Mayfield, where he married Roxie Corder in 1897. As president of the McMillan Sheep Company he took a leading role in Idaho wool growing. He headed the Idaho association and was on many national committees. Thomas McMillan was also manager of the Boise Stone Company that supplied Table Rock stone for many Boise buildings. He was a director of Boise City National Bank. Mr. and Mrs. McMillan had two daughters: Roxie, who married Ansgar E. Johnson, a photographer, and who became manager of the Idanha; and Irene, Mrs. Matthew Conley of Fresno, California. McMillan was an incorporator and director of the Idanha Company. He managed the hotel for many years before he died in 1953 at the age of eighty-eight. Mrs. McMillan died in 1961.

John McMillan plunged into the political and civic whirlpool almost as soon as he hit Idaho. More of a shaker and maker of public affairs than his brother, he followed his stint as Mayfield postmaster with a term as Republican kingpin for Alturas County and later Elmore County when it was created from Alturas. When he came to Boise he was elected Ada County senator for the 1907–1908 term. He also served as Boise postmaster from 1910 to 1914. In 1919 John McMillan ran for mayor. He came in first in the April election but did not get a majority. In the runoff he was defeated by Ern Eagleson. The margin was about six hundred votes.

Throughout his years in Boise, John spearheaded numerous enterprises in addition to postage, politics, and his directorship of the Idanha. He was the founder of the Intermountain Fair, president — like brother Tom — of the Idaho Wool Growers, and a policy shaper for the Commercial Club.

Another incorporator of the Idanha also had direct connection to the Corder ranch at Mayfield. Anthony McMillan, a brother of Tom and John, had a daughter, Mary, who married Robert Aikman at the McMillan ranch. The Aikmans had two children: Robert, later of Caldwell, and Mrs. Agnes Aikman Spofford, now living in Boise. Robert Aikman, Sr., was an Idanha founder.

That's the background of most of the personnel responsible for the Idanha. Without a bit of biography the cast of characters might be hard to understand. With historical and family connections, the development of an inn by these people becomes logical. The people were primarily livestock growers. They had a common background at Corder Station, and they were members of a generation dismayed by the approaching death of the Overland Hotel. They wanted Boise to have a hotel to take its physical place, if not its honored spot, in history.

The Overland was a hard act to follow. Idaho was born and raised in its parlor. Everybody who was anybody made a speech from its second-story porch. Men who spun the territorial wheels dined at its table and slept in its beds. They had their beards trimmed in its barbershop. They toasted the election of Abraham Lincoln at its bar and whooped on its torch-lit verandah when troops came back from the Bannock War. Social, financial, and political medicine bubbled through its halls.

Travel built the Overland. The most famous stage line in the West gave it purpose and a name. Ben Holladay's Overland Mail galloped across Idaho in 1864, linking the territory with Oregon, Utah, and California. B. M. DuRell and Company, which handled the Boise business, had its office at Eighth and Main streets. DuRell was also associated with C. W. Moore in a bank that became the First National. His interests included a general store that sold glass, paint, boots, dynamite, flour, and ham. The company had branch stores in Ruby City and Idaho City.

The Overland House was built in 1864 on the northwest corner of Eighth and Main. The corner had been known as

Idaho Historical Society

The Overland House was famous as the meeting place for stalwart citizens who carved a mining and grazing empire in the western wilderness.

Overland Station. The name stuck as naturally as bed to board. The frame hotel was two stories, with entries on Main and Eighth. The managers were G. Young, who had been in the hotel business in Salem, Oregon, and J. Mallory, a freshman at innkeeping, chosen by Young because he had a pleasant gift of gab.

Central Hotel, Seventh and Idaho, was built in 1865 and became the leading rival of the Overland. Territorial legislatures met at the Central. The fourth session nearly wrecked the place during a brawl about Yankee loyalty and legislative pay. Troops from Boise Barracks calmed the uproar.

The Overland was more decorous, concentrating on grand balls and fancy meals. Of one shindig in the early days *The Statesman* said: "The ball last night at the Overland House was all that could be wished for by devotees of Terpsichore. . . . The music was much better than we supposed could be procured in the territory. The assemblage of ladies and gentlemen was one of the most brilliant ever had in the country. At a little after 12 o'clock the gay and happy throng repaired to the dining room and partook of a splendidly gotten up and luxurious repast. Wine flowed freely, wit sparkled and beauty smiled. After supper the crowd returned to the ballroom and resumed festivities until an early hour. Proprietors Young and Mallory are entitled to much credit for the manner in which they have gotten up and conducted the pioneer ball of Boise City."

Among the entertainers at the Overland was John Kelly, a renowned fiddler, who for a few bucks a turn sawed off melodies, sang ballads, and cracked jokes. His assistant was an orphan Indian lad that Kelly had rescued from an attack by settlers. The lad added variety to Kelly's program by performing feats of contortion. One of his duties — which he did not need to do at the Overland — was to pull a rope that lifted a caged Kelly from the line of fire when shooting broke out in saloons at such places as Idaho City and Silver City.

The Overland also presented Professor Myers, "master

of magic, legerdemain, trickery, sleight-of-mind, and chemistry." Tickets were one dollar. Front seats were reserved for ladies. There were no ladies present on another occasion when the Overland was young. J. P. Bean, known as "Secesh Jimmy," had words in the saloon with James Buckley. They had a fist fight. The bartender chucked them out. They adjourned to another drinkery, where Buckley shot Jimmy dead.

In 1866 DuRell and William B. Hughes sold Overland House to J. W. Griffin and H. M. Ellsworth. Captain Griffin, a seafaring man in his youth, spent a decade or so expanding the reputation for the inn and building a name for himself as a Boniface nonpareil. Business boomed. There was a coach nearly every day to or from Salt Lake. They would have made it daily except for Indians and outlaws and broken wheels. Doctors, lawyers, merchant chiefs, drummers, and carpetbaggers stayed at the Overland. It was the business and social center. The gent who could take a corner room, have a bath in hot water, and smoke a fat cigar on the porch after a six-bit supper was either going places or had already been there.

One of the first things Cap Griffin did was renovate the inn from stem to stern. Hotel managers make that a rule. The new broom always sweeps the old furniture and wallpaper into the basement and crows about the improvement. It is an unwritten law of the business that the old must be chucked out and something new installed, even if the public doesn't give a hoot. Cap Griffin proclaimed that all rooms were being hand-finished, painted, and renovated. He said he was determined not to be excelled by any hotel on the Pacific Coast. He expanded bathroom facilities and provided easier access to a Chinese mystery on the alley. The Chinese shop was a combination laundry and medicine parlor, where rare roots and turtle blood were sold. There were rumors that the Chinese dealt in other merchandise, but nothing more violent than quarrels over wash jobs drew the attention of police.

The main entrance to the hotel was on Eighth Street. An

interior stairway climbed to the second floor, under carpeting worn threadbare by the boots of legislators, army officers, governors, and miners. The best rooms upstairs opened on a porch that extended the length of the building on Main and to the alley on Eighth. Rooms were unheated except for calories that trickled from the corridor. Each room had a kerosene lamp, washbowl, and pitcher. Water was cold. Warm water was supplied on request. There was a washroom and toilet down the hall. Prices at the Overland were high for those days. Board and room cost $5 a day in 1866. By the week, the price was $24. Meals alone were $17.50 a week. These rates were higher than those charged by the previous management. Griffin justified the increase by his expense for renovation.

Stories of Overland guests are legion. Everybody who lived or visited in Idaho between 1864 and 1904 stayed there at least one night — or heard so much about the place it seemed they had been there. One tale is about a miner who had been in the hills for months before he registered at the famous inn to ease his bones in the lap of luxury. During the night he left his room. When he returned he found his clothes and knapsack were gone. Wearing underwear and hat he trotted down to the lobby to report the robbery. The desk clerk quickly solved the problem. The miner had gone back to the wrong room. "By golly," he said, "next time I come to town I'll stay in a hotel with only one room."

Hart's Exchange, at the site of the Central Hotel, became a serious rival to the Overland in the 1870s. The name changed from time to time. At the third switch it was the Central — again or yet. To answer that threat, Cap Griffin renovated again. He tidied up from cellar to attic, served baronial banquets, and gave dances beyond the expectations of the most cultured denizens. He got back much of the trade the Central had been draining.

Most territorial goverors bedded at the Overland because it was handiest to the stage station and had the widest reputation. Some governors spent their entire stay in

Idaho Historical Society

The Central Hotel was one of Boise's first. Territorial legislatures met there.

Idaho at the Overland — for the reason that they didn't last long enough in office to unpack. One story has it that a newly minted governor walked up to the Overland bar, announced that he was the governor, and asked anybody who would accept the invitation to have a drink on him. There was a hush. Finally one man stepped up and allowed he would take a nip with the so-and-so. The governor did not remain long in Idaho.

Volunteers to fight Chief Joseph in the Indian war of 1877 mustered in front of the Overland. Orlando ("Rube") Robbins lined 'em up and headed 'em out. When the volunteers and the regulars, commanded by Capt. Reuben Bernard, returned in the fall they paraded past a reviewing stand at the Overland.

A military figure of greater stature parked his boots at the Overland in 1870. Gen. William T. Sherman, the commander who burned Atlanta and was largely responsible for the surrender of the South, came to Boise as chief of staff to inspect the barracks. He smoked half a dozen cigars on the porch, occupied the best suite, and said a few words from the balcony. He liked Boise, he said, and backed his words by retaining Boise Barracks. Prior to his visit there had been talk of closing the post. It was a good thing he didn't. Although General Sherman predicted that troops would not be needed because the Indian threat was nearly over, it was only a few years later that Custer was clobbered and three Indian wars swept over Idaho.

Hosea B. Eastman bought the Overland in October 1877 from Cap Griffin. In keeping with tradition he immediately remodeled. A year later his brother, B. M. Eastman, bought a half interest. The Eastman brothers maintained protocol by renovating again. They added a couple of brick sections, doubling the number of rooms. The famous verandah remained. It took a beating throughout the life of the hotel, not only in terms of the orations that flowed from its planks but from wayward traffic. Runaway teams and nervous saddle horses were forever breaking the posts.

As recently as 1890 the destruction was still going on. According to an account in *The Statesman,* a chestnut mare belonging to J. O. Baker jerked loose from a hitch rail. The attached buggy snagged a telephone pole. Parts of the buggy splattered the Overland porch, sending people into the lobby. Chairs and windows were smashed. The mare dragged remains of the pole and a garnish of Overland furniture to Boise River, where officers sorted out the ruins.

The horse incident had a counterpart of sorts at the Eastman Building, successor to the Overland. On a rainy afternoon a Boise man sought protection in the Eastman entry. That was okay except that he was riding a horse. And he rode the horse into the elevator. The operator objected. So did unmounted passengers. The horse didn't like the lift, either, and backed out as soon as possible. But the horse refused to return to the wet world. A cop came. The rider said something to his horse. The officer thought he was calling him a bad thing. Whether the description was meant for horse or officer or both, the cop marched horse and rider to the police station and filed a charge of parking a horse in a public building.

Getting back to earlier years, the statehood celebration in 1890 was a big day at the Overland. The porch was the reviewing stand for a "monster" parade with Gov. George L. Shoup in the Liberty car and Carrie Mobley as the first Miss Idaho. Notables, including Mayor James Pinney, looked out from folds of bunting that draped the inn from stem to stern. Bands played and firecrackers popped. In an event that had nothing to do with the Overland but is a tidbit of trivia, Boise and Pocatello played a 27 to 27 baseball game at the barracks. The game ended after ten innings because of umpire trouble. In a switch from common practice, players threw the umpires out.

The Overland called it quits in 1904, three years after the Idanha had opened. However, the march of time had taken its toll on the elderly Overland before the turn of the century. Comfortable and elegant as it had been in pioneer days, the inn was falling apart. Like so many institutions and individuals throughout history, it was out of step with change. It could not dance to the tune of a new era of sophisticated devices and social practices.

For its final blowout the Overland threw a party for pioneers on June 29, 1904. The Brothers Eastman and Manager E. W. Johnson invited oldsters to the homecoming. Anyone who had come to Idaho before 1869 was considered a pioneer. The cutoff date was determined by the fact that the railroad reached northern Utah that spring. Scores of old-timers flocked to the banquet. Frank Coffin was toastmaster. Remarks were offered by Jim Hawley, W. Goulder, Judge J. W. Huston, and Dr. T. H. Calloway. A. L.

Richardson got a prize for having arrived in Idaho the earliest. He said he got here in 1843. Nobody tried to top that. The homecoming ended with playing of "Home Sweet Home" and "Auld Lang Syne." There was scarcely a dry eye in the house.

Wrecking crews leveled the old Overland shortly after the last hurrah. In its place the Eastman Building rose. Originally intended as a hotel, the proprietors changed their minds. For one thing, Boise by that time had the Idanha. For a second thing, there was need for more office space in the heart of town. The Eastman Building was occupied for many years by drugstores, tailors, a book store, and many lawyers, physicians, and insurance agencies. Creaking in the joints and leaky in its plumbing, it was nominated for oblivion by the Boise Redevelopment Agency in its early eagerness to create a mall or two. Friends of the Eastman rallied. The structure was spared the wrecking ball. Significant bits of its entry arch were preserved by the Idaho Historical Society. The rest of the building is empty, except for ghostly whispers of its past and memories of the Overland Hotel.

The Idanha stepped into the picture three years before the Overland locked up and threw away the key. The ranchers from Mayfield and their associates knew that a big chore was ahead as they determined to fill the vacancy.

The site they chose was as much in the heart of Boise as the Overland. The northeast corner of Tenth and Main had been occupied some years earlier by a Presbyterian church, the first of that denomination in the city. The church was at Tenth and Main from 1878 to 1893, when it moved to its present quarters on State Street between Ninth and Tenth. The first minister, serving the original church, was the Reverend J. F. Knowles. The Reverend Joseph Barton was also pastor at an early period.

The site had a religious flavor. Talton ("Scotty the Terrible") Scott, a stagecoach bandit, was caught hiding under the Baptist church in the spring of 1876. Arthur Hart, director of the Idaho Historical Society, locates the church at

Tenth and Main.* It was later the site of the Idanha. The Presbyterians bought the site from the Baptists.

Scott was transferred from the undercroft of the church to the Ada County Jail. He sawed his way out of the calaboose with a blade made from part of a banjo. Caught again, he was sentenced to seven years in the territorial prison. He escaped once more in 1877, first to a dugout on Table Rock where he left tools and leg irons, then to freedom. He was not recaptured. Scott apparently preferred a sandstone cave to religious crypts. He no longer trusted church basements.

What role the Presbyterian church had in the location of the Idanha is not known, nor is it important. However, the McMillans were Presbyterians. What is more noteworthy is that Peter Sonna, also a Presbyterian and one of Boise's leading businessmen, owned most of the Main Street frontage on that block. When the church moved, he expected to extend his opera house, et cetera, to that corner. Instead, he sold to the Idanha Hotel Company and was closely associated with the development. Sonna was a banker and merchant. He was elected mayor in 1893 and in that office was a strong advocate of a bustling business core for the heart of Boise. That was, of course, long before BRAs and concepts of malls in the same vicinity.

One of the first public reports of the hotel's pending arrival was in *The Statesman* November 26, 1899. It said a hotel might be built at Tenth and Main, would be five stories, with 55 feet frontage on Main and 122 feet on Tenth. Materials would be cut stone and pressed brick. The architect was W. S. Campbell. He was enthusiastic about the design. He was particularly pleased that there would not be a dark room in the building. He arranged that a light shaft would extend from the first floor to the top, furnishing "all the light necessary."

The news story said the name would be Idanha. No ex-

---

*Hart has thoroughly researched Boise and Idaho history. He is the author of several books on Idaho and writes a weekly column for *The Statesman.*

Thomas McMillan, stockman, was a founder and long-time manager of the hotel.

planation was offered. Neither the owners nor the reporter hinted at the source. It was not long, though, before people remembered there had been an Idanha Hotel at Soda Springs noted for its drinking water, reputed to cure all manner of afflictions and make you feel good even if you were in robust health. Mineral water bubbled from many springs in and near Soda. For many years, continuing to current times, people have bathed in the water, filled jugs for drinking purposes, and tried it in gourmet cooking of wild game. As a mixer with alcohol it is of debatable quality. The water from some springs turns inky when blended with booze. Water from other springs stays reasonably clear but often gives the drink an unusual flavor. Because of these properties, Idanha water and its cousins were considered useful in mending the habits of drunks. Alcoholics who sopped up a jug or two of medicinal water combined with Ancient Headache were inclined to sign the pledge. Ironically, Boise's Idanha, up to its masthead in praise of bubbling waters, did not use natural hot water from the Boise springs.

"Idanha" appears to be a white man's creation. It stands for bubbling waters, healing waters, warm waters, sparkling waters, wrinkle-removing waters, and happy shampoo. Not only is the meaning anybody's grab bag, but the spelling is dealer's choice. You can spell it as one word, throw in a hyphen or two and a capital H, or spell it with an eyeball for a starter and a capital H for the finish. From start to the year 1983 the spelling has been a tossed salad, both in advertisements for the inn and in ads for other businesses using the same name.

The IDAN-HA

The first meeting of the stockholders that put the Idanha show on the road was held in late November 1899 in Room 5, Sonna Block. The men, who put up $5,000 each, were John W. Cage, Robert Aikman, John McMillan, James B. Morrow, and Thomas McMillan. All except Cage were ranchers. Morrow is listed in the city directory as a farmer living at 400 West Washington, but he had livestock interests. The McMillan brothers and Aikman were ranchers from Mayfield. Cage was the only hotel man in the bunch. He had been associated with E. W. Johnson in running the Overland House. Early in the spring of 1900 Cage separated from the Overland to devote his talents to the new hotel. As the man with hotel experience, he worked with the architect and with firms that sold hotel goods. None of the other board members knew anything about hotels except how to register and find the dining room. From his office in the Sonna Block, where brother Milton G. Cage practiced law before moving to Homedale, John Cage dealt with contractors, compared lines of crockery, and made plans for hiring clerks, chambermaids, and janitors. John McMillan, first president of the company, had moved to West Franklin Street by that time, so he was able to help the cause. At the same time he was busy, as was Tom McMillan, in growing sheep. The Idanha had to take its turn for attention.

The hotel was finished in December 1900. Construction took ten months. Cost was about $125,000. Hundreds of visitors poured in for the public opening January 3. A select group of personal friends of the stockholders had a party January 1. Corks popped. A supper of the finest food the market could supply was spread for the celebrators.

What guests of the Idanha could see from top to bottom was described in detail by *The Statesman*. There was a picture on the front page and a long article dealing with the comforting appointments denizens of the modern palace would experience. One of the extraordinary features was an electric elevator, said to be the first of its kind in the Northwest. It was powered by a fifteen-horse motor in the basement, covered with glass so the public could see it work. "The elevator," the story said, "is of handsome design by the Otis Elevator Company, one of the best elevator makers in the world."

When people finally tired of zipping from floor to floor on the elevator they could instruct the uniformed operator to let them off, and they could find refreshment at the bar. The men's bar, that is. There was a dining room or parlor for ladies on another floor reached by a separate stairway. The ladies, bless them, did not drink with gentlemen except in special quarters the Idanha took pains to provide in a discreet way.

The first floor was of terrazo — white cement and Italian marble, rubbed and polished. The Main Street entrance was a massive stone arch. Pillars supported a balcony that played a notable role in Idaho oratory. Brass rails led to the basement.

Above the safe in the first-floor office stood the "enunciator," a fabulous gadget that connected all 140 rooms with a bell system. When a guest wanted room service or the time of the next train he could get on the enunciator. A light flashed in the office. A clerk responded, enunciating as clearly as possible that a bellman would be up promptly with a pitcher of lemonade or that the train from Nampa was on time. Telephones were also available. A guest could obtain one for a daily fee.

The dining room off the lobby was thirty by sixty feet, with a large brick fireplace. On the second floor a parlor, twenty by thirty feet, connected to the ladies' entrance to the bar. The parlor had a banquet room that would accommodate small groups. It was connected to the kitchen by a dumb waiter.

An architectural flourish of which Campbell, the designer, and the management were unusually proud was a steel balcony from the second floor over Main Street. It was more than an ornament. On numerous occasions it was the platform from which oratory flowed and from which verbal sparks kindled patriotic fires in the hearts of Boise citizens. Several episodes concerning the balcony will be related later.

Only three rooms in the entire hotel were "inside," the mangement pointed out, meaning their windows did not open to the world. Even the bathrooms and toilets on each floor had windows. All corner rooms had bay windows. Some of these corner havens were suites, with private bath, writing desk in the bay window nook, and a pantry in which snacks could be prepared with assistance from the culinary staff. Everything was up-to-date in the Idanha as in Kansas City. As a matter of fact, architect Campbell visited Kansas City when he toured the country before he decided on the design for the Idanha. He said he looked at nearly all the modern hotels between Boise and New York.

Foundation walls were of hard sandstone from John Krall's quarry, held together with cement. Two carloads of cement were needed. Krall's quarry was northeast of Boise above the Krall orchard. Table Rock quarry, later managed by Tom McMillan, was farther east. The Krall quarry is now surrounded and nearly smothered by residences perched on slopes affording views of the valley.

Plumbing, heating, and electrical work, the dedication

article said, "are the acme of perfection." There was steam heat, with a radiator in every room. The Idanha had seven fire escapes of steel rungs on cable ladders, rolled up when not in use. Steam for the radiators was generated by a five-ton boiler in the basement not far from the elevator well. Opening-day guests had a peek at that, too.

The management noted that roomers could turn on lights by pushing pearl buttons that shone in the dark. There was no groping for switch or string, as in some unidentified inns.

E. J. Pratt, a traveling man — also known as drummer or salesman — was the first person to register. He was from Salt Lake. Partly because of the distinction, the Idanha Hotel was soon designated as an official library of United Commercial Travelers. About twenty Boise businesses chipped in to buy books for the salesmen. They were general-interest books, not confined to salesmanship. The cover of one recently found in the hotel basement is "The Hound of the Baskervilles," by Conan Doyle, a tale suited to the use of the hotel by detectives during the Harry Orchard excitement and appropriate to whispers of modern ghosts on an upper floor. The library for commercial travelers no longer exists. Nor does the national brotherhood. Airplanes and computers have silenced the drummers. Knights of the grip are gone with the wind.

Ladies and gentlemen attending the grand opening of the new hotel had moderate temperature for their buggy rides or walks. The coldest was eleven degrees above zero and the warmest twenty-four above. Not a heat wave, but normal for Boise at that season.

Boise Commercial Club congratulated the Idanha. The note was signed by W. E. Pierce, president; C. A. Anderson, treasurer; James A. Pinney and Nathan Falk, directors. John McMillan, also a director, humbly abstained.

Opening of the hotel was the top story of the day for Boise's press. It was undercut only by the attempted suicide of Edward Rice, a barfly from Wallace who was awaiting execution at the penitentiary for killing a storekeeper a year earlier. Rice cut his throat in a death-row cell. For several hours it seemed he had done a thorough job, but Dr. George Collister patched him up. When he was whole again and had been taken through the legal thicket of appeals, delaying actions, and hocus pocus ad nauseum, he was pronounced fit for hanging. He was hanged November 30, 1901, with C. E. Arney as warden. A statement of the crime that led to the gallows said that Rice was traced to the fatal bludgeoning of Matt Mailley in his cigar store by a handkerchief left on the dead man's face. It had Rice's laundry mark.

The Rice episode was a leading topic of conversation among people who pretended horror and said they wouldn't listen to another dreadful word — at least until they hurried up the private stairs and begged for further details. The delayed execution was on the front conversational burner during the next Thanksgiving season, when the Idanha spread one of its famous feasts.

The Idanha began advertising January 6, 1901. *The Statesman* carried the first notices. The *Capital News,* an afternoon paper for many years, also came in for space. The Idanha styled itself "The Only Modern Hotel in Boise, Costing $125,000." Rates were $2 to $4. The hotel was on safe ground in saying it was the only hotel in Boise costing $125,000 and probably without error in calling itself the only modern hotel in town. It was the most recent and the most costly. There were numerous other places to stay the night, but none were in the financial class of the Idanha, and none could boast an enunciator or an elevator.

Here's a catalog of hotels trying to share customers:

The Overland, E. W. Johnson, prop. "Idaho's Best Known Hotel." Venerable and about to close.

The Capitol, Main between Eighth and Ninth, Frank Blackinger, mgr. "The Leading Hotel in Boise." It had been a popular inn for years and still was patronized by many old-timers who had known Blackinger at Silver City. Its most noted furnishings were a pair of Sevres vases from France that stood at the ends of the bar. They were about

An advertisement for the hotel in 1901

four feet tall and were said to be worth a fortune. A few years after the advent of the Idanha, the Capitol gained national fame as the place where Owen Wister wrote much of *The Virginian.* To keep visitors out of his hair he left his key in the box downstairs and told the clerk he was away for the day.

The Pacific, G. B. Smith, prop. Successor to the Bancroft. "Best Family Hotel in Boise." Rates, $1.00 to $1.25. The quarter was for a bath.

The International, 912 Grove Street, I. W. Pfost, prop.

"The Only $1.25 hotel in Boise. All white Help and Everything Neat and Clean."

Lesser boardinghouses and joints of unsavory repute were abundant then and later. The Idanha was the jewel. It was preferred by the fastidious and affluent. The Idanha was the political center and the watering hole for stockmen. Governors and legislators made it their headquarters during legislative sessions. Gov. Frank Gooding lived there during his two terms, 1905 through 1908. Other governors stayed there from time to time. Frank Steunenberg made it a practice to take a room at the Idanha while working on cattle business and newspaper matters after his term in the statehouse, 1897 through 1900. He was almost bombed to death there. Details of what happened will be given later as this narrative unfolds.

As for businesses in Boise when the Idanha took its bow, there were many that are still more or less familiar in 1983. W. S. Whitehead Drug was in the midst of holiday sales of such standard apothecary goods asrfume, traveling cases, and cameras. Whitehead's occupied a corner of the Eastman Building for many years.

Alexander's, Seventh and Main, was going through a grand opening of a special department and having a closing-out sale of some lines of men's clothing. Ties were 25 cents. The closing-out sale continued at least eighty-two years.

Ladies of the Episcopal church had a "gypsy camp" in the Levy Building near Sixth and Main. The site of the bazaar raised eyebrows. The Levy property was a notorious red-light district — a bizarre place for a religious bazaar.

The Statesman, a morning daily published by Calvin Cobb, was seventy-five cents a month, delivered. The paper was home owned and operated. The *Capital News,* an afternoon publication, sold for less than *The Statesman* because it came out only six days a week. The *News* was involved, even then, in liaison with a chain. Absentee influence was generally regarded by the news fraternity as a cardinal sin.

Idaho Historical Society

Frank R. Gooding made the Idanha Idaho's political and social center when he was governor. He lived there.

For visitors and home folks, the Natatorium was a major attraction. Streetcars ran nearly every hour to and from the Nat. On some days the traffic was more frequent. Guests at the Idanha could board a car at Tenth and for a nickle be deposited at the plunge or get a transfer at Broadway for a tour of the entire city. As a growing city of about nine thousand people, Boise was regarded as the regional hub as well as the pot of gold at the end of a rainbow painted by developers. The post office in the Sonna Building handled a lot of in-and-out mail about irrigation, railway, and stock raising.

Having done what was considered a commendable job on the French-chateau-style Idanha, architect Campbell drew plans for a Chinese temple on Idaho between Seventh and Eighth streets. It was three stories, with a sanctum for select brethren at the top and shops on the lower floors in which the public was welcome to spend money. Fong Suey, a citizen, put up the building on his land in order to obtain a valid title. The building commonly known as the Chinese Masonic Temple, cost $12,000. During years of alleged tong wars, at widespread intervals from about 1909 through the 1930s, tales were told of tunnels joining the temple with noodle houses on South Seventh Street and as far west as a laundry on Eleventh and Idaho. Sinister Orientals in black jackets and soundless slippers materialized from manholes, baring three-inch fangs and swinging knives that would slice an ox. These hair-raising creatures gained support from parents who didn't want their boys and girls prowling Chinatown. Police boosted the campaign by arresting a Chinese now and then in a dugout. The opium dens were factual. It is unlikely, however, that they were a subterranean Maginot Line. Their primary purpose, except for opium smoking, was for Chinese outhouses. That was made clear about the turn of the century when a drayload of beer sank over its hubs into a quagmire on Idaho Street.

At one time the Boise Chamber of Commerce was headquartered in the Chinese temple. While it was undergoing remodeling Ned Harlan, secretary, found the entrance to what was thought to be a tunnel. A wall was broached in the basement, disclosing a cave. Excitement died as quickly as it started. The cave proved to be a pipeline for water supply, sewer, electric cable, and telephone wires. It went back about six feet and ended against a cement basement, around and through which the utility fixtures continued. There was no indication that Chinese had ever dug a tunnel there. The same was true of basements along Seventh and Front when several Chinese buildings, including the joss house, were razed to make room for Boise's redevelopment center. Tumbleweeds and acres of empty space now mark the vicinity. No tunnels were found. Scientific diggers did uproot a few Chinese dishes, vintage circa 1930.

There is more linkage between the Chinese temple and the Idanha than a common architect. Chinese and the Idanha had a confrontation and a flowery reconciliation. Stand by for later revelations; loose ends will be tied in due time. Architect Campbell joined Charles Wayland in partnership. When Campbell went to Scotland in 1904 Wayland took over.

The Idanha made its entrance on the athletic scene in the spring of 1901. Ira King, a bellhop, and Ray Pendleton, a barber in a shop not connected with the hotel, announced they would ride a bike to Buffalo in June, expecting to cover the 2,300 miles in 25 days. They would pump a Tribune tandem. On the return they would visit their old stomping grounds in Missouri.

The excursion on a bicyle built for two was not intended as a challenge, but the Overland Hotel considered it was. Even though the Overland was a tottering senior citizen it insisted it had young blood left to carry its banner. Len Anthony of the Overland staff volunteered to ride a Rambler tandem to Buffalo over the same course. He would race King and Pendleton if he could find a partner. His mate turned out to be John Dial of the Idanha. Such a combination took the wind out of the competition. Whichever pair arrived first, if ever, the Idanha couldn't lose. The race started June 1 and disappeared into the wide blue yonder. Biking turned out to be very tough. The contestants abandoned the idea somewhere in Wyoming.

John McMillan, president of the Idanha company and chairman of the fair board, had other business on his mind. He had to find a new site for the fair because the old one had been taken over by other concerns. As an upshot of that difficulty, plus a conflict with Spokane over dates for the Intermountain Fair, there was no state fair in Boise in the fall of 1901. A minor league street fair was substituted.

On the occasion of its first Fourth of July, the Idanha was honored with a band concert in front of the hotel. The Columbia band played there and also at the Capital and Overland. Main Street from Sixth to Tenth was roped off, allowing pedestrians only. A crowd of about five thousand took part in and cheered greased-pole climbing, a pie-eating contest, footraces, and bicycle races. In the evening there was a parade to the Nat for speeches, fireworks, and dancing. The band "discoursed sweet music."

Just a year after the Idanha opened, John Cage terminated his lease as operating manager and sold his stock to the company. He felt he was unable to continue after the death of his wife. E. W. Schubert, assistant manager, became manager. Schubert had a prominent role in the operation of several Boise inns.

The elite of Idaho's political leaders gave a banquet at the Idanha late in 1901 honoring George L. Shoup, former governor and former U.S. senator, who had just retired as Idaho's national Republican committeeman. The banquet room was filled by fifty men. Judge George H. Stewart presided. William E. Borah called Shoup "the lion of the north, the sachem of the party, a benevolent personality of calm and considerate judgment." W. B. Heyburn and James F. Ailshie added tributes. George H. Roberts, a double general as a military commander and former Idaho attorney general, praised Shoup for his honesty and sound decisions.

Just as the Idanha was getting out its tinsel for Christmas, it was thrilled to serve a member of the British nobility. Lord Fingall from County Meath, Ireland, an aristocrat, was installed in the finest suite on the second floor. Lord Fingall — Arthur James Plunkett without the trappings — was in Idaho as a representative of General Kitchener, British commander in the Boer War, South Africa. The British needed cavalry horses. Lord Fingall and his deputy, Harold Sessions, had heard that Idaho might spare a few. They were right. They bought a lot of stock in Owyhee County from Kitty Wilkins and enough to fill immediate needs of the remount commission from several other ranchers in Idaho and Eastern Oregon.

His lordship talked freely about horses but steered clear of international matters. He was careful not to make any comment that might be interpreted as reflecting the policies of Her Majesty's government on the attitude Americans should take in the Boer rebellion. On other subjects he was up to the eyebrows in Irish blarney. He said the quality of Idaho horseflesh was splendid but was far exceeded by the beauty and charm of Idaho women, whom he found to be among the most delightful in the world. To the surprise of nobody, particularly Boise females, he was given a grand Christmas at the hotel and in homes of Boise's aristocracy.

About the middle of January newspaper advertisements began to list E. W. Schubert as Idanha manager. Cage had been out of the picture for at least a couple of months, but it took time to bring amenities up to date. Idanha rates were $2 to $4 as before. There was no remodeling of the building, just of the management.

Room rates were only one example of what the dollar would buy in the winter of 1900–1901. Among the favorite places to buy groceries was the IXL at Ninth and Main, just a block from the Idanha. Prices: sixteen pounds of rice, $1; sardines, five cents a can; ham, eleven cents a pound; oranges, twenty cents a dozen; candy, ten cents a pound; three pounds of coffee, fifty cents. Good cigars were a nickle at Abe Frank's "The Parrot," opposite the hotel.

Other things were happening as Boise ventured into the twentieth century. Traveling actors put on dramas at the Columbia Theatre. The Galbraith Drug Store was sold in March 1901 to C. O. Ballou and James B. Latimer.

More than thirty members of the Chicago Commercial Club visited Boise that spring. Traveling by train they had Pullman quarters so did not need hotel rooms. They visited the statehouse, the Nat, the Idanha (for a peek at the elevator), and tree-lined residential areas. A newspaper item said several millionaires in the group were favorably impressed and might invest in Idaho. Chicago and Idaho capitalists were encouraged, another story said, by the hope that Boise might soon have automobiles. One had already made a trip over the mountains in Custer County. Very soon they were likely to be all over the place.

One of the reasons for optimism about Idaho's growth was progress on the New York Canal. Dirt was flying on the job that would water more than twenty thousand acres. Eighty men and forty teams were scooping earth.

A project that didn't do so well was the Idaho Midland Railroad. The line was to run from Boise to Butte. Approximately one hundred Japanese were brought to Boise to start building the bed and laying track. They got a few miles short of what was later to be Arrowrock Dam. It was a far piece from there to Montana. Thomas W. Bates, promoter, encouraged the Boise Commercial Club to open its pockets. Club stalwarts were reluctant. Bates then delivered what was called an ultimatum: unless he got a bundle, the deal was off. A public meeting at the Columbia Theatre raised about $9,000. A few weeks later it went up to $20,000. In view of the distance to Butte that ante seemed short of adequate. The railway was not built. Sections of the Japanese right-of-way were used a dozen years later when a railroad was constructed to Arrowrock to transport construction materials for what was to be, for a long time, the highest dam of its kind in the world, at 351 feet.

Another company, the San Francisco, Idaho and Montana Railway, incorporated in 1905 to build a line from San Francisco to Butte via Boise. Headquarters were to be in Boise. One million dollars worth of stock was issued. Construction of that railway, like that of its predecessor, is still under advisement. Far under.

The IDAN-HA

The Idanha was up front and flying high at one of the twentieth century's fanciest social events. The inaugural ball in 1905, when Gov. Frank R. Gooding took office, was something to tickle the giblets of the gentle sex. John McMillan was secretary of the committee planning and running the extravaganza for the governor, who was then moving into a suite at the Idanha for an extended stay. Manager Schubert was a member of the committee. The sleekest and finest transportation on wheels was shined and oiled to carry the honored guest and his party to the Natatorium. Buggies and carriages trotted from Tenth and Main to the swimming palace, where the pool was covered with flooring to accommodate dancing and munching.

The grand march lasted more than half an hour. All state officials were there in their best raiment. Hanging baskets of Chinese style were supplied by Dr. Chin Man Sui. Japanese and Chinese lanterns lit the scene. Two score waiters ministered to guests. Festivities began with a fanfare of trumpets. At halftime a buffet lunch was served to one and all. Nearly eight hundred tripped the light fantastic. Street cars set a record of 1,304 passengers for the day, to and from the Nat.

The ladies were careful to look their best. Their dresses were described by *The Statesman.* Mrs. Borah wore pink peau de crepe, accordion pleated, a bertha of duchess lace, and flower garniture in her hair. Mrs. McMillan wore a robe of black embroidered net. Mrs. Frank Blackinger was charming in embroidered mull. And so the catalog went on. The outfits of virtually every female on the premises were diagnosed by Mrs. Eva Hunt Dockery, society editor for more than a third of a century. Male getups were not discussed. The standard, from which there was no departure, was soup and fish — boiled shirt, tails, and glistening patent leather shoes. Silk hats were in full bloom.

Mrs. Dockery said the ball was a sensational success.

Idaho citizens in general and men who had attended an Idanha tribute to Governor Shoup a short time before the Gooding era were gratified that they had honored the grand old man while he could appreciate it. He died just before Christmas 1904 at the age of sixty-eight. A memorial in the legislature said, "His public career was characterized by devotion to duty and his public and private life to perfect purity." A committee met in the suite of Governor Gooding to launch plans for a statue of Shoup in the Senate Gallery of Fame in Washington, D.C. The statue was installed. It is visited today by throngs from throughout the nation and particularly appreciated by residents of his state.

Party politics were set aside on many occasions at Boise's leading hotel. Although proprietors of the Idanha were vigorous Republicans, they recognized laudable qualities in members of other parties. Democrats celebrated Jefferson Day at the Idanha banquet room in April 1905. In those days the party had not linked Jefferson and Jackson for one blowout, as is the practice in modern times. A "toothsome menu from oysters to coffee" — as the newspaper put it — was served to a crowd of Bourbons, chiefly supporters of W. J. Bryan, who was then ascending into the party firmament and was later to be a visitor at the Idanha during one of his runs for the presidency. Luminaries of the Democratic faith were in mellow voice. Judge C. Blake was toastmaster. Speeches were given by Judge K. I. Perky, Judge John Rice of Caldwell, and Moses Alexander, then identified as a former mayor of Boise. A few years later he became governor.

J. D. Flenner toasted "all Democrats," taking the diplomatic route through an assembly of gentlemen leaning in different directions in their ambitious travels to public office. The assembly noted with relish the presence of Avery Moore, a Republican reborn a Democrat. He was petted as a lost lamb returned to the fold. In response to that cuddling he said kind words about the sage of Monticello. The entire proceeding took place in the dining hall, decorated with portraits of Jefferson and Jackson and under the eye of a stuffed American eagle.

The war between Russia and Japan had repercussions at the Idanha. Gan Tackihaur — or so it appeared on the police blotter — celebrated the 1905 victory of his native Japan over the Russians in a major battle. He surrounded a generous portion of saki and took to the street in jubilation. He stopped at the Idanha in search of companionship. Finding there were no visiting Japanese on the register (hardly unusual because persons of that race were seldom in the city) he trotted down Front Street knocking on doors to see if he could raise a Russian to poke in the snoot or a Japanese countryman with whom to hoist another nip of rice wine. Sad to say, he sought too long and in vain. Between one and two o'clock in the morning he was mistaken for a burglar and fired upon by a householder who was not at all concerned or amused that Japan had kicked the stuffing out of the Czar.

Police collared Gan. At the station he explained that he had been seeking employment when he was so rudely interrupted. He said he had knocked on a Front Street door in hope the resident needed a houseboy or a cook. The middle of the night was hardly the time for such an interview. Neither was the liquid diet on which he had prepared himself for the job market.

Fates conspired in favor of Gan. The police judge who

listened to the particulars next morning fined Gan $5 and turned him loose because it was St. Patrick's Day. What better time for a broth of a boy from old Tokyo to dance a jig for Galway Bay? Saints preserve us and all lads of the Rising Sun!

The Idanha had scarcely opened its doors in 1901 before a cloud of regional competition formed a few miles west. Col. W. H. Dewey, mining titan of Owyhee County and a major influence in the Thunder Mountain boom, decided to put up a hotel in Nampa that would make the Idanha look like a shack. Not only would his hotel be superior but it would be further evidence of his alleged intention to make grass grow on the streets of Boise. Whether he ever made such a statement is conjecture, but it is commonly accepted as close to the truth. (Colonel Dewey did not live until 1983, when he could have seen tumbleweeds and thistles on business streets of downtown Boise's gaping monument to the Boise Redevelopment Agency.)

Even while the Idanha was under construction there

The Dewey Palace was built at Nampa as a rival to Boise's Idanha. The Palace is long gone. The Idanha survives.

Idaho Historical Society

Idaho Historical Society

Col. W. H. Dewey, mining magnate, built a hotel at Nampa to compete with the Idanha.

were rumblings from Nampa that the Dewey Palace would outstrip the McMillan inn. When the Idanha said it was using about twenty carloads of cement, Dewey said his hotel would take twice as much. He further stated that the $125,000 the Idanha was said to cost was peanuts. His palace would set him back at least $200,000. Maybe the total would be half again that sum. He was putting the best materials and decorations available from around the world into his hotel. It would be a masterpiece for weary guests to enjoy and a jewel for architects to use as a yardstick for craftsmanship. His hotel was built. It was most of the things Colonel Dewey anticipated, allowing for a parental brag here and there.

The Dewey Palace was opened to the public on New Year's Day 1903, just two years after the Idanha began. A special edition of the *Nampa Leader Herald* said it was "the most magnificent hotel in all Idaho." It was three stories, 125 rooms, some with fireplaces, a steam laundry, restaurant, and its own electric plant. Reporters said the hotel stood out "like a castle in a barren waste." A summary of the event by Annie Laurie Bird in *Boise, The Peace Valley* (Caxton Printers, 1934) says descriptions used such phrases as beautiful, grand, harmonious tints, expert Chicago decorators, handsome tiled floors, large screened verandahs, summer resort — and what more could be desired? The account of the dedication says steam heat worked to satisfaction, the bar was well patronized, and the menu provided for a variety of tastes. Colonel Dewey gave a grand banquet and ball late in February, termed by one reporter as "a magnificent carnival of pleasure."

Colonel Dewey delighted in his pleasure dome. He did not have long to enjoy it. He died three months later.

A notable visitor to Idaho in May 1903 was President Theodore Roosevelt. It is sometimes said that he stayed at both the Idanha and the Dewey Palace. That is not factual. He may have strolled through both lobbies or looked at the hotels from a street procession, but he did not spend a night in either city at that time. He stayed on his special Pullman railway car.

Roosevelt the First did stay in Boise a few years later, when he was a candidate of the Bull Moose party. At that time he took another look at the Idanha from the street while he was the honored guest in a political parade. He then made a speech at the Pinney Theatre and returned to his open automobile. He was a guest of Judge Charles F. Koelsch, who provided the top-down car. The judge decorated the back seat with an American flag. In getting out of the car, Roosevelt caught a shoe in the flag, ripping a ten-inch hole. Judge Koelsch repaired the damage himself, darning the gap with typical male stitches. The mend is rough as a plowed field. It is distinctive and revered. The ten-by-six flag flies on every holiday at a house on Krall Street, clumsy mend and all. It was left to the proprietor of that house when the judge died.

Superiority of the Dewey Palace over the Idanha or vice versa is a matter of opinion. Plenty of constituents supported opposite sides. Time worked on behalf of the Idanha. The Dewey Palace faded in the 1930s, as did many inns throughout the country. Both the Dewey Palace and the Idanha suffered in the 1950s and subsequently, as motels popped up. Finally, the Dewey Palace turned in its keys. The hotel was razed in 1963. Nearly twenty years later the Idanha is still in business. Chandeliers from the Dewey Palace were hung in the Idanha.

The IDAN-HA

The arrival of a Colorado miner in 1905 began a chapter of Idaho history that put Boise on the front pages of newspapers throughout the nation. Harry Orchard (also known as John Dempsey, Albert Horsley, and T. S. Hogan in his infamous career as a paid killer) took a room at the Capital Hotel, believing that Frank Stuenenberg, former governor, stayed there during his frequent trips to Boise from his Caldwell home. Orchard's line of work at that time was a combination of insurance salesman — a job he had tried for several months in the midwest as Tom Hogan — and livestock buyer. What Orchard knew about beef or mutton was very little. He did savvy milk cows, having worked in a dairy in his native Canada. Ewes or steers were all the same to him, in what he expected to be an interview with Steunenberg. Whichever it was the governor was buying or selling, that would be Orchard's dish. The meeting did not come off. Steunenberg was not at the Capital Hotel; he wasn't even in town.

Orchard presently found out that the governor stayed at the Idanha because it tended to live up to its advertised slogan — "livestock, political and social center." If Orchard had paid more attention to information given him a short time earlier, while he was at the Saratoga Hotel in Caldwell, he would not have made the mistake. People there had told him Steunenberg preferred the Idanha; but he fumbled the ball. When Orchard switched to the Idanha he was delighted to find that Steunenberg had checked in.

It didn't take Orchard long to learn Steunenberg's room number and his daily habits. Orchard had a way with ladies. He became chummy with a chambermaid. She knew a great deal about Steunenberg's schedule, such as when he ate his meals, when and where he was most likely to be during the day, and when he would return before dinner. On the basis of that blueprint the dynamite man lugged his black bag to Steunenberg's room and rigged a bomb that would tear the governor apart about a quarter after five.

The clock attached to the bomb ticked so loudly Orchard was afraid it would be noticed by other people. He was concerned that his friend, the chambermaid, would look under the bed at the wrong time and be blown to bits. Killing governors was okay. Chambermaids, no. She was a cute little trick. Orchard scampered upstairs and disconnected the device. The chambermaid never knew what had been going on. Neither did Steunenberg.

Subsequent events have been detailed many times. Two of the best accounts are in *Murder Out Yonder,* by Stewart Holbrook (the Macmillan Company) and *Debaters and Dynamiters,* by David Grover (Oregon State University Press). Each account has references to the Idanha. The story of the chambermaid is part of Idanha lore, passed down from generation to generation on the alleged authority of room clerks and bellhops.

Why Orchard didn't take another crack at Steunenberg at the Idanha is explained by Holbrook. He says Steunenberg left on some sort of business trip that was to last about three weeks. With nobody to blow up, Orchard went to Portland to take in the sights of the Lewis and Clark Exposition. Then he took a little trip to the upper reaches of Puget Sound, where he hoped someday to buy a farm near the Canadian border and go in for a little smuggling. The

Idaho Historical Society

Harry Orchard rigged a bomb in the Idanha to kill Frank Steunenberg. He disconnected it for fear of hurting a maid.

matter of smuggling is reported by Holbrook as taken from Orchard's confession a couple of years later.

In December 1905 Orchard resumed stalking the former governor, following instructions from the head men of the Western Federation of Miners to "tear him loose." The federation had the hatchet out for Steunenberg because he had called on the militia to stop mine violence in the Coeur d'Alenes in 1899. The Bunker Hill and Sullivan mine (which closed in 1982 because of the general financial crunch) was in the thick of the turmoil.

Using the name of T. S. Hogan, Orchard again put up at the Saratoga in Caldwell. Professing to be a sheep broker, he spent most of his time in his locked room perfecting a ten-pound dynamite bomb that would go off when a string pulled the cork from a bottle of acid. Holbrook notes that such a bomb would have made rubble of the Idanha. He also says the hotel had the "fine flavor of the McKinley-Roosevelt period, retaining a pioneer charm of which Boise, with its interesting tonnage of glass block and chromium, should be glad."

Shocking events that took place at Caldwell are told by Holbrook:

"He had already looked over the lay of the land, and considered it the best bombing chance he had seen. The Steunenberg home was the only house on its street. There were several members of the family, so Orchard studied their comings and goings, and one evening in mid-December he knew that Steunenberg was downtown and almost ready to start home on foot. Taking the bomb, Orchard set it beside the only path that led to the front of the house and then stretched a stout cord from the bomb to a small stake he drove on the other side of the path. Half an hour later he watched while the ex-governor started for home. The minutes passed, very long and quiet. There was no explosion. Investigation later that night indicated to Orchard that the intended victim has stepped over the cord without suspecting its existence.

"Steunenberg left town the next day and was gone almost two weeks, but on Saturday afternoon — it was December 30 — Orchard, who was playing cards at the Saratoga bar, saw him come into the hotel lobby. Orchard quit the game. He went across the street to the post office and returned by way of the hotel lobby. He saw that Steunenberg was still there, talking with two men. But it was now after six o'clock and he was sure that Steunenberg would soon start home for supper.

" 'I went up to my room,' Orchard says, 'and took the bomb out of my valise. I wrapped it in a newspaper, put it under my arm and went downstairs. Mr. Steunenberg was still in the lobby. I went outside and hurried as fast as I could to his residence, and laid the bomb down close to the gatepost. I then tied a cord to the screw eye of the cork and ran it around the picket of the gate. I had it fixed so that when the gate was opened it would jerk the cork from the bottle and let the acid run out and set off the bomb.

" 'I fixed it so that even if he did not open the gate wide enough to pull the cork he would still strike the cord with his feet and this would do the job as well. I brushed some snow over the bomb and hurried back to the hotel.'

"Next, as the reader knows, Orchard passed Steunenberg when the man was about two blocks from his home, and the explosion occurred at about the same time Orchard reached the Saratoga. After a quick drink at the bar, he went to his room. It was here and now that he made his slight mistake. Let him tell it in his own words.

" 'I was going to take some things out of my room and throw them away. There were some bits of dynamite, some pieces of fuse, several giant caps, and a bottle or two of acid. I emptied the acid into the sink and put the bottle in my side pocket, planning to take it downstairs and throw it away. It wasn't two seconds after I put that bottle in my pocket when a flash like a pistol shot rang out in the room and the coat was nearly torn off my back.'

"Little wonder. What had happened was this. In his pocket Orchard had a spare detonator or two, and giant caps. The bottle he had just put in his pocket was not quite

Idaho Historical Society

Senator William E. Borah was a familiar figure at the Idanha

empty. A drop or two of acid remained. It dribbled out, reached the caps, and off came the old Rocky Mountain dynamite man's coat, blown, as you might say, by his own petard."

Steunenberg died in his home about twenty minutes after he was bombed. Orchard was arrested January 2, 1906, and jailed at Caldwell. He presently confessed a series of crimes, including the bombing of Steunenberg, to James McParland, head of the Denver office of the Pinkerton Agency.

Immediately on learning of the tragedy at Caldwell, Governor Gooding, living at the Idanha, dispatched a special railway car of officers and executives to the scene. He also offered a reward for capture and conviction of persons responsible. The reward eventually reached $15,000.

The Idanha, because of its gubernatorial suite and because it was the scene of the earlier visit by Orchard, quickly became the hub of feverish activities dedicated to catching the murderer and revenge against the inner circle of the mining federation, believed to be at the bottom of the homicide. Governor Gooding approved extradition of William D. Haywood, Charles H. Moyer, and George Pettibone from Colorado. They were whisked to Idaho in February on a special car. They remained in jail at Caldwell and Boise until trials were conducted in 1907 at Boise.

The way the defendants were "smuggled" to Idaho was the subject of long and bitter debate before and during the trials. The defense called it kidnapping. Court decisions supported the action of extraditing officers. The issues are still tossed around in judicial decisions. Right or wrong, the three men Idaho thought most responsible for Orchard's dreadful deed were in custody of the Gem State. The Idanha buzzed with a hubbub of lawyers, detectives, and reporters. The place was packed. Rooms were at a premium. Because of the delicate nature of the case, bodyguards protected the leading characters. Outsiders curious about the drama, but having no official part in it, found it difficult to tell the real performers from hardware salesmen.

Boise got notoriety. The assassination horrified the country. Interest was increased by the involvement of organized labor. Champions of the working classes, who believed miners were getting a bum deal, protested the charge against Haywood, Moyer, and Pettibone. Mine owners and management in general favored vigorous prosecution. It was a classic confrontation of capital and labor. For Boise, an agricultural center far removed from the mining pits, the experience was perplexing. Being in the limelight of national headlines was a heady experience. The glamour was offset by anxiety for the safety of public officials who might be singled out for further attacks by the mining federation.

Soon after Orchard was moved from the Canyon County jail for safekeeping at the state penitentiary, platoons of journalists and detectives swarmed over Boise. The immediate cause was the report that Orchard had sung loud and long to James McParland. Officials of the mining federation said Orchard had done no such thing. They insisted that McParland had trumped up a yarn to back up the charges against Haywood, et al. McParland stuck by his account, letting out bits and pieces of the entire alleged confession. Orchard was isolated from the press. For some time after he was transferred to the state prison the only people he saw were his jailers and the detective. Most of what he was to say was kept for his day in court as a witness for the prosecution. Isolation of Orchard was as much for his protection as for judicial procedure. Although opinion was strong that Orchard was being used as a tool of capitalism and that words had been put in his mouth, there were fears that some hotheads might blast Orchard if they could reach his cell.

While the most sensational trial of the decade took shape, Boise earned attention for other reasons. Growth of the community caught the eyes and ears of regional cities. Either because of the Orchard business or because substantial growth of the inland economy was worth exploring, about seventy-five Portland businessmen came to Boise by train. They were wined and dined by the Commercial Club, taken on the usual tour of attractions such as the Idanha, the Nat, and the statehouse. Leo J. Falk and Judge J. H. Richards delivered speeches of welcome, along with expressions of confidence that Portland and Boise would be working partners for the further success of the West.

Two weeks later a similar delegation from Salt Lake visited Boise for almost identical treatment. Salt Lake, it seemed, had heard of Portland's overture. Really, the Salt Lakers said, Boise should look to the Utah capital for its genuine friendship and support. Boise blushed at the wooing from so many suitors. It flung itself at none, keeping cordial relations with all but playing no favorites.

Clarence Darrow of Chicago came to Boise in the early stages of preparation for the Haywood trial. He was noted even then as one of the most able defense attorneys in the business. He championed underdogs and was a loyal supporter of labor.

Where he lived in Boise is a matter of conjecture. Quite likely he spent part of his time at the Idanha. A corner suite on the second floor is nominated by the present management as the place Darrow occupied. A desk in the bay window is said to have been the place he wrote many of his notes. The king-sized bed now in the bedroom was definitely not where Darrow slept. It is a waterbed.

Thin lines of reports from that period indicate that Darrow left the downtown scene in order to avoid the commotion of reporters and witnesses. He is believed to have taken a room in a boardinghouse. He was somewhere other than the Idanha when he was treated for an abscessed ear during the trial. The pain nearly caused him to drop out of the case. Treatment eased the condition, however, and he was able to continue — to a conclusion that was music to his ears and his reputation.

At the outset of his Boise period, Darrow was very low key. His first appearance was at the Columbia Theatre. A large crowd turned out for what they expected to be a lively preview of trial fireworks. Darrow said nothing about Orchard, Haywood, or labor. He delivered a scholarly lecture on Walt Whitman.

That bit of diplomacy set him up in the community much better than his reputation had indicated. He gained respect for his judgment. He was not then afflicted by the bad ear. The earache, some have suggested, was brought on when he heard what Orchard was singing.

The Idanha did not get the business of housing and feeding the Haywood jury. That would have been improper, because the men who would decide the momentous issue could not be exposed to the hubbub in the lobby and in the upper halls no matter how bailiffs shielded them. The jury, when finally selected after protracted examination, was quartered at the Konrad house, Sixth and State streets, not far from the old Ada County Courthouse where the trial was conducted. A spokesman said they liked it fine. They approved of the cook.

Although the Heyburn trial was the major attraction in town, it was not the only event in the public eye. Just as Darrow was warming up in his skirmishes with Borah and Hawley, Sells-Floto Circus pitched its tents on Thirteenth Street. During a recess called by Judge Fremont Wood, four bailiffs escorted the jury to an afternoon show as guests of the management.

Belle Chamberlain, state superintendent of public instruction, and Louise Johnson, state librarian, gave the area a scare during the same week by nearly drowning in the Snake River. The cable broke on a ferry they were riding a short distance above Shoshone Falls. The accounts that were rushed to Boise (and were no doubt expanded in conversations at the Idanha) said the two women had been "snatched from the jaws of death."

Other news revealed that the Sells-Floto Circus had run into a spot of rough going in Magic Valley. The day before the Boise show a tiger got loose at Twin Falls and killed a girl. Harry Tammen and Fred Bonfils, circus owners and publishers of the *Denver Post,* were sued in federal court for $5,000. It was clearly a big season for interesting suits.

Idaho Historical Society

Clarence Darrow, famous defense attorney, lived at the Idanha during part of his stay in Boise during the Haywood trial.

In spite of such sidelights, the Haywood trial held center stage. Harry Orchard was the main performer. For more than six days he confessed not only to killing Governor Steunenberg and having a part in an abortive scheme to blow up the governor of Colorado but also to a leading role in the murder of at least a score of men connected in one way or another with activities the miners' union thought detrimental.

Miss Ethel Barrymore heard part of his tale. She was more impressed by Orchard than by the questions Darrow frequently interposed in his effort to make Orchard seem a colossal liar. Because she was an actress unaccustomed to interruptions while on the stage, it may be that she resented the lawyer's breaking the thread of a hair-raising tragedy. Miss Barrymore wanted the show to go on without the distractions of Darrow's scathing sarcasm.

During her visit in Boise Miss Barrymore refrained from comment on the case. A *Statesman* reporter noted that she occupied a seat inside the rail — a section usually reserved for members of the bar — and that "her unheralded presence soon drew a crowd." Interviewed later at the Idanha, most likely by Eva Hunt Dockery, she still dodged questions about the trial. The reporter fell back on a description of her clothes. The story said she wore "a chic suit of tan linen with a touch of blue on the collar and cuffs, and a large black hat of straw. She said the jury looked exceedingly intelligent."

Miss Barrymore not only upstaged Darrow and Borah but Professor Hugo Munsterburg, a doctor of psychology at Yale who came to Boise on assignment for *McClure's Magazine* to study the main characters. His presence was hardly noted at the time, but later he received pages of copy because of his analysis of Orchard's personality. He concluded that Orchard was telling the truth — but not the whole truth and nothing but the truth.

Miss Barrymore offended some of her Boise admirers a few days later while she was appearing in a play at Spokane. She said she thought Orchard was a very honest man. She liked his appearance, his attitude, and his straight-forward response to difficult questions. She said she believed he was a repentant sinner, who, in effect, had been born again. However right she may have been, the interview did not go down well in Boise. Noses were out of joint because she had not spoken her piece for Boise papers. In the second place, her comments infuriated attorneys for the defense and a wide circle of citizens who believed Orchard cooked up his account of a plot by officers of the mining union to rub out scads of capitalists.

Orchard's confession covered a multitude of sins. Day-by-day portions were printed by newspapers in Boise and in many parts of the country. Edited versions of the whole horrifying account are contained in *Confessions and Biography of Harry Orchard,* published by the McClure Company, New York, in 1907, and *Harry Orchard, The Man God Made Again,* by Orchard in collaboration with LeRoy E. Froom, published by the Southern Publishing Association, Nashville, Tennessee, in 1952. There are, as mentioned earlier, treatments of the case in books by Stewart Holbrook and David H. Grover.

Orchard testified he had been a hit man in Colorado, California, and Idaho. He claimed he moved in with his little black bag whenever there was a strike or a threat of a strike at a mine. He was handy with dynamite, acid, poison, and other tools designed to help people shuffle off the mortal coil. He admitted at one point that he had killed about sixty people. That count was suspect because there was no accurate tally of victims in a train explosion in Colorado. But give or take a few here and there, Orchard was responsible for more than a score of fatalities. Before he made a career of blowing up people, he deserted his wife and child. With such a background it is reasonable that his reputation for truth and veracity, in or out of court, was less than overwhelming.

A part of the confession of special interest to Idahoans tells about Orchard's attempt to kill Fred Bradley in California. Bradley had been manager of the Bunker Hill and Sullivan Mine in the Coeur d'Alenes in 1899. Orchard's story runs, in part:

"Haywood said Bradley was at the head of the mine operator's association of California and he said they were raising an immense fund to drive the Federation out of the state, or words to that effect. He also said they had sent Steve Adams and Ed Minster to California to get Bradley, but they did not accomplish it. I told them I would go down and try it. . . . Pettibone got me a ticket and a new grip and I took the train for San Francisco. . . . I went by the name of John Dempsey. In San Francisco I stopped at the Golden West Hotel. I located Mr. Bradley's office and also his residence. His office told me Mr. Bradley had gone on a trip to Alaska and would not be back for three months. I wrote a letter to Pettibone and told him about this. We had a sort of cipher to write by so no one could tell anything about it if it fell into their hands. I also told him in this letter to send me $100.

"I had bought ten pounds of dynamite to make a bomb with and got a room only a few doors from Mr. Bradley's flat. This room was on Washington Street about a quarter block away, but on higher ground, and my windows were about on a level with the Bradley flat. I could look right over into it. There was a little grocery store and a saloon on the opposite corner from Mr. Bradley's residence, and they used to buy their groceries there, or part of them. I used to loaf in the saloon a good deal, and spent quite a bit of money with this man. . . . The girls that worked for Mr. Bradley used to go over to the store every day and the proprietor gave me an introduction to them. I took one of them to the theatre once and found out when Mr. Bradley was expected home. I stayed until he did come home. I went by the name of Berry there.

"After Mr. Bradley came home, some time in October, I learned his habits pretty well. He used to leave his residence about eight o'clock in the morning. They lived in a big three-story residence flat that had six families in it. There was a big archway at the entrance and the flat was built out flush with the sidewalk. They all went in at this archway, but each family had a private entrance to their apartment. I had figured a good many ways how to do away with Mr. Bradley the easiest and not get caught. I had stood across the street in front of the entrance to his residence with shotgun loaded with buckshot, and tried to catch him coming home at night, but it was not light enough to tell him from the rest, so I was getting sick of staying there, and Pettibone had sent an answer to my last letter asking him to send me $500, to call it off, and did not send the money.

"I was getting desperate for I thought they took advantage of me, not sending the money because they thought I dared not come back to Denver. I made up my mind to go back and show them. I knew Haywood, Moyer, or Pettibone dare not refuse me money if I asked them personally.

"The desperate and horrible means I conceived at this time to carry out my plan to kill Mr. Bradley I would gladly withhold and let die in my breast. But I feel that perhaps I owe someone a duty they may have been blamed for this and wrongfully accused. I feel it my duty to make this known as I have promised God I would write the whole truth of my wicked and sinful life, and not try to favor myself. I have made this attempt several times and it has required no small effort on my part to write some of these things.

"There was an empty house with a flat roof just behind the apartment where Mr. Bradley lived, and there were stairs up from the back way on the outside of the apartment. I went up these stairs and got on the roof of the vacant house and waited there until the milkman brought the Bradley's milk, which was a little before daylight. I knew he left this milk in bottles as I had watched before. I had a little powder of strychnine made for each bottle and raised the paper cover and emptied one of these in each bottle and stirred it up a little, and pressed the paper cover back again, and left and went back to my room. I figured the girls would serve Mr. and Mrs. Bradley breakfast first and that they would get the poison first. I could see the kitchen plainly from the window of my room but could not see anything unusual there that morning.

"I did not get up until ten and sometimes later, and then I usually went down to the little bar to get a drink and sat there and read the morning paper. This morning I did the same and noticed a bottle of milk standing on the back bar. I asked Guibinni, the bartender, if he was serving milk, or drew his attention to the bottle in some way like that. He began to tell me about this milk and wanted me to taste of it. He said he had tasted of it and could feel it in his throat yet. He told me the girls over at Mr. Bradley's had brought that bottle over and wanted him to take it down and have it analyzed as they believed there was poison in it. He said it was bitter as gall. Now I never knew before that strychnine was bitter, but it seems the cook had tasted of some of this, found it was bitter, and told Mrs. Bradley, and then they came over to Guibinni's place to get some more milk and cream for breakfast.

"After this failed, I got a bomb ready. I bought a piece of five-inch lead pipe about a foot long at a plumber's, and put wooden ends on it. Then I hammered one side flat so it would lie straight without turning over. I cut a piece out of the other side and turned back the flap and fastened a little vial on this, so that when you filled it with sulphuric acid and you pulled out the cork the acid would run into the hole in the pipe. Then I filled up the lead pipe with about five or six pounds of No. 1 gelatin and put some caps and sugar and potash on top of this and opposite the hole in the lead pipe so the acid would fall on them. Then I planned to hitch a little string to the cork of the bottle and fasten the other end of the string in a screw-eye in a door so when you opened the door it would pull out the cork and set off the bomb.*

"I practiced with this while I was making it in my room

*An apparatus of this type was used later in the Steunenberg assassination. The devilish device at the Idanha was rigged to a clock in a different system.

so as to see if the cork would come out of the bottle instead of moving the bomb. I had the dynamite in but not the caps or acid and I tried it by fastening a screw-eye and string to my closet door. It worked all right. But one day I left the screw-eye and the string and the cork on my door and went downtown and forgot about it. When I got home I thought how nice a trick it would be to leave that thing there so I thought the woman who kept the house must have seen it when she cleaned up my room. But she never gave any sign that she saw it.

"After that I watched what time Mr. Bradley usually came downstairs in the morning and how soon after he ate his breakfast. I was on a level and could see them at their meals. I noticed Mr. Bradley came downstairs soon after he had finished breakfast so I had to guess that he would be the first one downstairs. In order to be sure he would be at home I called him one night and told him I was from Goldfield, Nev. and had some mining property and wanted to raise some money on it; and that he had been recommended to me and I would like to make an appointment. He said he would be pleased to meet me and talk the matter over. I asked him if he could make it the morning after that, and he said he could, at nine o'clock. I did not want to try the bomb next morning as I was not ready.

"The next night I fixed a screw-eye in the door of his residence and watched in the morning until he went to breakfast. Then I took the bomb, hooked a cord over the screw-eye and laid a mat over the bomb. It looked like a small parcel as I had done it up in a paper. After I left the bomb I took a car and went downtown and rented another room. . . . About four in the afternoon I bought an evening paper to see if there was anything about the bomb and there was not a thing. I felt pretty uneasy as I knew if it had not been exploded it would be sure to be discovered and I might have been seen there. I took a walk on the West side, out of the busy part of the city and felt pretty miserable. The world looked more desolate than it ever had before. I could not see much for me to live for. I went to a restaurant and got another paper. There was a picture of the explosion and a full account of it. This paper said Mr. Bradley would probably die or at least lose his hearing and eyesight. They gave the cause of the explosion as leaking gas fixtures. It said Mr. Bradley had lighted a cigar and ignited the gas. . . .

"Pettibone was well pleased with the news, but said it was hard luck that Mr. Bradley did not die. He got well after a while and was neither deaf nor blind."

Further chapters of Orchard's testimony in court (subsequently rephrased for his book) presented play-by-play details of the Steunenberg bombing, including the unsuccessful attempt at the Idanha. It all made rich grist for newspapers and for the scores of guests at the hotel, where affairs bubbled in keeping with the traditional meaning of Idanha.

The IDAN-HA

The Haywood trial, at which Orchard was the major witness for the prosecution, lasted a couple of months. Most of the first month was devoted to selection of the jury. Among men on the roster of potential jurors were J. B. Morrow, a member of the Idanha board of directors; Capt. J. Yates, building developer and hotel proprietor in another part of Boise; and Albert Beck, a member by marriage of the Corder family of Mayfield and a sometime operator of the Pacific Hotel at the northwest corner of Ninth and Idaho streets. All were excused. The list of 124 witnesses for the state included E. W. Schubert, manager of the Idanha, whose registration books established that Orchard had been there at the time Orchard confessed he had tried to blow up Steunenberg. Although there was credible evidence that Orchard was telling the truth in most of his testimony, so many doubts were cast on his revelations that independent facts were essential.

Orchard took the stand two days after the start of the actual trial. He began telling of his revolting crimes on June 5 and kept telling for many days. He started with his employment as a miner at Burke in 1899 and continued through the business at the Idanha and the ultimate assassination of Steunenberg at Caldwell. Newspaper articles said he appeared healthy, having recovered from ailments that shrank his weight and gave him nightmares.

Within a day or two after Orchard disclosed that his real name was Albert Horseley and that he was born in Canada in 1866, the press corps dug into his background. Accounts said he was the black sheep of a respectable family.

Just before Orchard took the stand he spent a night in the office of James Hawley, one of the leading lawyers for the state. Orchard was released from the state prison for the occasion. Guards were on hand at the office and in the alley below. Orchard had not been tried for the assassination at that time. He was in protective custody at the prison rather than in the Canyon County jail.

Excitement sprouted next day when a strange object was found by a paperhanger on the street near Hawley's office. Police thought it might be an infernal machine of the Orchard type prepared and left by enemies of Orchard. Members of the mining union were suspected of trying to silence Orchard by whatever means necessary. The mysterious thing, stuffed in a paper sack, was about the size of a shotgun shell. The tin casing was plugged at one end. The object was saturated with a sticky fluid. The interior was left unexplored. Suspecting the contents might be explosive, Chief Ben Francis gingerly disposed of the thing. Whether it might have gone off and blown somebody to bits or was an innocent firecracker was never determined. Orchard was noncommittal. If he was alarmed he didn't show his fears to Hawley or others at the court. Nobody in the mining fraternity claimed parentage of the device. Orchard continued his confession with no apparent change in his denunciation of federation officers. A little dynamite, or threat of dynamite, did not intimidate the dynamite expert.

Something that did disturb Orchard was a surprise guest in Hawley's office. He was James Peabody, former governor of Colorado, whom Orchard had tried to assassinate several years before. Orchard and Steve Adams, another giant-powder specialist for the Western Federation of Miners, had been selected for the mission because they were experienced. Governor Peabody had been nominated for destruction because he had called out troops in Colorado to put down rioting miners, a situation similar to that of Steunenberg in Idaho. Despite elaborate plans the bombing was a flop. For all his touted ability as a powder expert, Orchard often bungled assignments. He gummed up the first try at blowing up Bradley in California, leaving evidence all over his hotel room. He also missed the boat at the Idanha when he geared his bombing clock to the wrong hour.

Of all the people Orchard might have expected to meet in Boise while he was telling the grisly tale of his black past, the last was Governor Peabody. An account in *The Statesman* said: "Orchard's cheeks paled and a visible tremor shook his frame."

Substance of their conversation was not revealed by the two main characters or by Hawley. Governor Peabody, staying briefly at the Idanha and then moving to the Hawley residence, kept a cool silence with reporters. The significant purpose of his trip to Boise was to satisfy attorneys that Orchard was telling the truth regarding the Peabody incident, thereby reinforcing the veracity of his shocking confession.

A further bomb scare alarmed Boise Valley. A janitor at the *Meridian Times* found a bundle of dynamite under the back steps. The immediate thought was that miners had intended to destroy the *Times*. The weekly paper, however, had not been outspoken on the trial. It had reported news as it happened. The *Times* had no labor axe to grind, nor was it throwing thunderbolts for either side. As the shock of finding a batch of dynamite subsided, cooler heads reasoned that if the miners or mine owners or anyone else was about to bomb a newspaper it would not be the *Meridian Times*. There were larger fish at closer range.

Management of *The Statesman* and *Capital News* took quiet precautions. The protection quickly proved unnecessary when it was determined that the dynamite at the

Meridian Times was left by a stump blower for safekeeping because he was caught in a storm. He retrieved his cargo and went about his blasting business, highly embarrassed by the notoriety.

People poured into Boise from all points to attend the Haywood trial, along with its sideshows. Another governor joined the congregation when George Sheldon of Nebraska led a delegation of eighty Omaha businessmen to Idaho in a special train. The reason, he said, was a business trip to express goodwill to Boise. Reporters noted that the goodwill took about an hour and the rest of the time was spent in the courthouse. What the visitors were selling there was not understood. Orchard was not in the market for civilian goods, unless it was hacksaws. He had used up about all the dynamite he needed. Attorneys and the presiding judge were not interested in buying wholesale groceries, kitchen ranges, harnesses, or button shoes.

Another visitor who gained the public ear in more straightforward action was a divine from Brooklyn, the Reverend Hewell Dwight Hills. He arrived in the first place to observe Orchard and others, and in the second place to deliver a sermon or two on crime. He did not pass judgment on Orchard's sincerity, leaving that to his Maker. The Reverend Mr. Hills did say the Haywood case "aroused more profound interest than any trial since the prosecution of Aaron Burr for treason."

Important though the Haywood case was, Boise did not neglect lesser offenses. During the very week the Reverend Mr. Hills was in town two men were arrested for using obscene language in the presence of women. They were kept in jail overnight to cleanse their vocabularies. In another part of town a couple of young men were arrested for reckless driving. They were sprinting around the polo field on bicycles. Another young sprout was collared for drunken riding a horse on the sidewalk near Seventh and Main.

The press had plenty to cover, major league and trivia. But the pace was too slow to satisfy some hotshots. Reporters from big dailies — mostly Chicago and eastward — took to improving their copy. They sat in their Idanha rooms and whopped up tales of astonishing deeds that had not happened nor ever would happen. Members of the local press were amazed to read in the lurid journals in Boise that all sorts of monkey business was going on that they had not been aware of. For instance, there was a front-page story in a journal of wide circulation stating that Orchard had slipped out of the prison one night and placed enough dynamite around the statehouse to blow it to smithereens whenever he flipped a certain switch in his cell.

There were also yarns about secret meetings of miners with Chinese to line tunnels under Boise's business district with enough powder to toss Boise to Table Rock. The intriguing, and mostly imaginary, tunnels under Boise fascinated visiting scribes then almost as much as they have through decades.

More than merely inventing whoppers, some of the reporters distorted testimony. Words were put in the mouths of witnesses who said no such thing. Prejudice was rampant. Accounts were so slanted to one side or the other that facts were hard to decipher.

Some members of the press were shocked by the deceptions of their brethren. They published corrections of the most glaring hogwash and pleaded for objectivity. One of the disturbed reporters was Joel L. Priest, representing a Salt Lake paper. As a thoroughly competent and dependable journalist he was disgusted at the trend to headline hoopla. He resigned as a reporter and took a position with the Union Pacific Railroad. He soon became general agent for Idaho, a role he filled with distinction for many years.

Religion had a significant role in the Orchard episode. The dynamiter wept on the stand as he told of his hope for salvation. The first push toward acceptance of Christianity was applied by McParland, the detective. Ordained ministers of the gospel had their part in helping the sinner stick with his avowed convictions, but it was the Pinkerton agent who started him on the path of repentance. Orchard told about it on the stand and expanded on his conversion in his book. The accounts say that McParland put such a scare into Orchard that he trembled with fear. Punishment about to be applied by the court, McParland advised his prisoner, was not a patch on what was eventually in store. For the first time, apparently, Orchard got the wind up about hell and damnation. He sobbed that he was prepared to take his earthly punishment but could not abide the wrath of Almighty God. Unless he made a clean breast of his multiple murders and other destruction of the Commandments, he believed he would roast eternally. The advice he got from McParland was reinforced by Hawley, Borah, and others. He left the witness stand eager to start his reformation under the guidance of professional clergy. His sincerity was accepted by several ministers and some members of the Steunenberg family. Eventually he became a religious man, able to use his physical talents in jobs at the state prison.

In his first interviews with McParland, Orchard virtually slammed the door on repentance. He said he didn't have a chance. Much as he might wish for a better existence in the hereafter, he was such a black-hearted monster nobody in heaven would give him a second look. McParland, who knew a thing or two about scripture, told Orchard how David committed murder by sending Uriah to the thick of battle where he was sure to be killed, leaving his wife to the carnal appetite of David. That story seemed to hit home. McParland followed it with the New Testament account of St. Paul holding the cloaks of men who stoned Stephen to death. If those characters in the Bible could do such miserable things and be forgiven and respected in later life for their noble deeds, there was reason for Orchard to believe he might have a chance.

The Very Reverend Edwin S. Hinks, dean of St. Michael's Cathedral, assisted Orchard in his spiritual reformation. Dean Hinks wrote the introduction to Orchard's book of confessions.

He writes, in part:

"As I comprehend the transformation of Harry Orchard from reckless criminality to a penitent willing to tell the truth, I feel that the world should understand that his change of front was not in the order of religious conversation, then moral perception, leading to confession. No, it seems to me the order was first physical, second moral, and finally religious. He was wretched behind stone walls, lonely as cut off from freedom and old associations. Hence, he fairly craved the sympathy he got in unburdening his mind to McParland. He told me that at first he told only a little of the truth, and that several days passed before he divulged in full. . . . He told me that though he had never doubted the existence of a God, and positively believed in a future state, still he thought himself to be beyond forgiveness.

"He sat from week to week brooding on his lost condition, convinced that a murderer could not be forgiven. He had read the Bible sent to him from the east, searching for light when I first met him. Almost immediately he came to the point on which he desired my expression of opinion, based on the words of Scripture: Was he, a murderer, shut out from hope of God's forgiveness? I explained to him that neither in the Old Testament nor in the New Testament was there a single word to preclude a penitent from an honest approach to God, whose forgiveness and pardon are full and free. I have only sorrow, not contempt for those who make distinctions in the Ten Commandments. . . . I believe in the love of a forgiving God and as the Scripture defines God in the one word, "love," I firmly believe that radical change was as possible for Orchard as for the thief on the cross of Calvary. . . .

"What a genuineness is discerned in the fact that when the devils 'Hogan' and 'Orchard' had gone out of Albert E. Horsley, he believed implicitly in the devotion of that noble, Christian wife whom he had deserted nine years ago in Canada with a seven-months-old baby in her arms. I have seen some of her letters and have personally met her, and I am sure that nothing but the superhuman power of Christ can account for the calm, sustained spirit in this true, earnest wife, who has suffered so keenly since the truth came to her.

"My conclusions as to the honesty and present truthfulness of Albert E. Horsley are based on my experience with human beings. I would not know how to make a psychological test, according to the accepted scientific method, but I was gratified that when Professor Munsterberg of Harvard had spent eight hours with Orchard, using every art known to his profession, he pronounced him to be normal, honest, frank and straightforward. In conclusion, I would say that any kind of publicity is objectionable to me, and that my association with this entire matter is not of my seeking, but accidentally came in the line of my duty. . . . My deepest sympathy lies with the honest wage earner, possibly in a large sense from a fellow-feeling. I pray for the day when capital and labor will be fair with one another. . . . It will never come until Christianity enters into the souls of those who pay out money as well as into the souls of those who receive it, and the rugged manhood of the Carpenter of Nazareth is accepted as the only standard worth considering."

A part of the confession of Orchard that is often overlooked is that he forgave the jury for acquitting Haywood in spite of Orchard's testimony that was calculated to send him to the scaffold or at least to a long term in prison.

"I have told the truth in this awful trial," Orchard wrote. "God alone has given me strength to openly confess these crimes. My conscience is clear. I know I have done what is right and made all the earthly restitution that is within my power. Mr. Haywood has been acquitted. I can truthfully say I would far rather see him acquitted than hanged. I believe the trial will do much good, as I do not believe these leaders of the Federation will take a chance again with anyone for the sake of revenge upon those who oppose the organization. My earnest prayer in closing this awful tale is that it will be the means of stopping this kind of work forever."

Meanwhile, back at the Idanha before Haywood was

acquitted, the press continued to wring every drop of high-powered juice from the proceedings. The outpouring of florid copy gushed to all corners. Some of it, as before, was manufactured out of whole cloth and fantasy in hotel rooms. The turmoil reached such a stage, according to Boise writers, that scribes from afar were interviewing one another under the mistaken impression that parties of the first and second parts were privy to important items of testimony. Detectives were behind every keyhole, although McParland said none of his Pinkertons were at the hotel. Reporters swarmed the halls, dodging and baiting each other. Some of the copy they filed with their managing editors fairly curled the telegraph paper.

One gentleman of the press, more objectionable than most, got his exodus from brother reporters. The writer, a correspondent for *Appeal to Reason,* a red-hot labor journal that appealed mostly to bombers and skull busters, was charged with rape of a young lady at the Idanha. While legal papers were being prepared in connection with his bail and arraignment, he picked up his typewriter and skedaddled for Denver. Charges were dropped in October, after the Haywood-Orchard excitement had cooled. The girl in the case was a resident of Pocatello attending school in Boise. Her mother, related to a labor leader in the Gate City, said the charge was trumped up. It may have been. Certain reporters, not impressed by stories of the trial in *Appeal to Reason,* may have played the trumps.

THE IDANHA – Built 1900

This etching by Elizabeth Mowrey is printed with consent of the artist and the Idaho Historic Preservation Council, Inc.

The IDAN-HA

Comic relief from the tension of the trial was provided by Hogan the Stiff — by no means to be confused with the Hogan of Hogan-Horsley-Orchard string of aliases. Hogan the Stiff was one of Boise's most colorful and imaginative drunks. Alcholic stupor was his normal condition. Jail was his major residence. He wasn't a mean drunk; he liked to be sociable. He had wit. He enjoyed jokes, even though most of them were on him.

In May 1907, when the Haywood trial was gaining steam, Hogan took no interest in court affairs, having spent the bulk of his adult life on the wrong side of a magistrate. He marched down Main Street to the Idanha corner, lifting his derby to one and all, bowing in courtly manner to retrieve a cigar butt or two from the gutter. He paused at the door of a shop next door to the Idanha. He pricked up his ears and scowled. A phonograph inside the shop was making noises that did not appeal to Hogan the Stiff. He shouted a protest. The phonograph went on with its noise. Hogan wobbled to the rear of the Idanha and armed himself with a chunk of brick. He gave the phonograph one more chance. He was ignored. Hogan flung the brick through the window, crippling the musical instrument.

Hogan expressed no remorse. To the contrary, he was delighted. He explained to officers that the infernal device was making fun of him, talking about him in a language he did not understand and offending his senses with diabolical racket. Hogan went to jail for several days and paid a fine of a few dollars, pungled up by anonymous benefactors who were suspected of sharing Hogan's opinion of popular tunes of the era.

Hogan the Stiff thrust himself into the news frequently. He was always up to something that left him temporarily in durance vile. On one of his adventures, several months after he knocked out the phonograph, he had a part-time job at an undertaking parlor. He was a sort of night watchman and janitor. After sweeping the floor and tidying up the premises to his satisfaction, he felt he needed a rest. Taking a flask of restorative medicine with him he snuggled down in a casket. Next morning the proprietor and some customers selecting a coffin were startled when Hogan rose from his silken bower, lifted his derby, and bid his audience a cheery good morning.

The Idanha, along with much of the population of western Idaho, was shocked in the summer of 1907 by a shooting at the hotel. This was a vintage year for Boise! The Haywood case would have been plenty of excitement by itself. Now the city had a new thriller, the Hedges-Whiteway scandal, which threatened for a time to shove Haywood and Orchard back to page 10.

It was the afternoon of June 23. Henry Hedges, a civil engineer from Caldwell, shot A. S. Whiteway, a contractor associated with Hedges on a construction job. Information supplied by investigating officers said Hedges resented Whiteway's attention to Mrs. Hedges. The front-page newspaper account said Hedges took Whiteway up to his hotel room — Number 5 — where Mrs. Hedges was spending the day. Scarcely pausing to say how do you do or good afternoon to his wife, Hedges fired several shots with a .32 calibre handgun. Four hit Whiteway. All were from the rear. The first struck Whiteway in the neck. Others struck his shoulder, arms, and leg. Whiteway collapsed on the floor, where he was left for dead. Dr. Springer, summoned by police, examined the corpse and pronounced the patient alive and likely to recover. Unaware that his target was still breathing, Hedges told officers he had intended to kill his wife as well but lost his nerve. Three of the bullets missed Whiteway. They drilled a wall in the corner room of the parlor floor.

As the shooting began, Mrs. Hedges shouted "Don't kill him."

"It's done," he replied. Lines and action had overtones of MacBeth, with roles reversed.

Hedges calmly surrendered to Officer Tim Kelley near the elevator. Action was proceeding quickly. It was only a few minutes from the first shot to the arrest. An ambulance drove up for Whiteway. He was conscious as he was put aboard. He complained mostly of a wound in the leg. The hole in his neck, not far from the spinal cord, did not appear to be the leading concern. Whisky was administered. About fifteen minutes after the shooting he was at St. Luke's hospital.

D. C. Scott, a witness for the state in the Haywood case, took Hedges to the police station as a volunteer to assist Officer Kelley. Scott said Hedges told him he took Whiteway up to his room to shoot him. He suspected Whiteway had been uncommonly friendly with his wife. Scott also said Hedges turned the gun on Mrs. Hedges, dropped it, and blurted: "I don't have nerve enough to shoot you, too." He lighted a cigar on the way to the police station, appearing to custodians to be composed and confident.

Charles F. Koelsch, county attorney, filed charges against Hedges of assault with intent to kill, pending severity of the wounds. If Whiteway died it would be murder. Koelsch found himself in a welter of unexpected work. He was already deeply involved in the Haywood case. The last thing he needed on his plate was another serving of capital crime. Hedges hired Frank Smith of Caldwell to represent him.

Further particulars surrounding the shooting came out gradually. The Hedges and the Whiteways, it was reported, had dined together the previous evening at Brand's Cafe, a classy restaurant in the basement of an office building at Ninth and Main streets, since torn down in early stages of Boise's downtown development. Whether Hedges and Whiteway had words at dinner was not revealed. There were whispers, however, that Hedges had mentioned to friends that he was not at all pleased by Whiteway's attentions to Mrs. Hedges.

Where was Mrs. Whiteway during the battle? She was in the Overland Pharmacy eating an ice cream soda. She had been to a baseball game at Riverside Park and was waiting for a streetcar at the soda fountain when she learned her husband had been shot. She hastened to his bedside. Her shock was eased somewhat when the doctor said he was likely to live.

Given the same information, Hedges showed no emotion. He puffed another cigar. He declined comment to the press, leaving statements to his attorney. Mr. Smith wasn't saying anything, either. When Whiteway was out of danger, Hedges was released on bail.

The case was put off several times. The county attorney was up to his neck in more pressing business. The victim soon was ambulatory. He was released from the hospital earlier than originally expected. All wounds were healing.

Papers and proceedings were filed from time to time, with no ostensible progress except to meet requirements of the judicial system.

Minutes of the court — dimly legible on microfilm — show that a trial was scheduled for the spring of 1908. It did not come off. Another minute says the case against Henry Hedges was dismissed for lack of evidence; a material witness was not available. Who the witness was is not known. Speculation is that it was the shootee, who wanted to hear no more about his alleged transgressions or the retribution of a jealous husband.

The froth of the triangular incident having subsided,

public attention returned to Haywood and Orchard. There was a brief distracting interlude when a window peeper, said to be a man in women's clothing, frightened women at a Washington Street residence. Alarmed by the screams, he or she was not apprehended.

The IDAN-HA

Much of the Haywood trial was taken up by the Orchard confession. Darrow's job was to tear it apart. He was in the difficult position of branding Orchard a murderer ripe for execution and at the same time insisting that Orchard and officers of the mining federation did not do the things to which he confessed. He scorched Orchard as a murderer, admitting much of the confession as fact but singling out portions detrimental to Haywood as fiction. The press was divided. Most of the local scribes said Darrow failed to shatter Orchard's horrendous tale. Papers more favorable to organized labor proclaimed that Darrow was destroying the confession.

Biased stories in the press meant little to the outcome. That was up to the jury. The verdict of not guilty was brought in on a Sunday morning, July 28, 1907, after twenty-one hours of deliberation. The trial had lasted eleven weeks. *The Statesman* said the verdict "was a surprise to everyone." The jury was reported deadlocked 10–2 all night.

There was no celebration at the Idanha. Reporters and detectives left town quickly, after filing final stories. The end of the trial was particularly gratifying to armed men who had taken shifts in an upper room of a rooming house just north of the area that was later Hotel Boise. Jim Hawley, son of Gov. James Hawley, a leading lawyer for the prosecution, recently recalled that deputies with rifles were stationed in the attic, where they had a clear view of the courthouse grounds and were prepared to take action if violence erupted.

Jubilant forces of the mining federation kicked up their heels in Denver. Reaction on their behalf was quiet in Boise. The federation announced that a special train would take the defendants back to Colorado. It was appropriate, the miners said, because Haywood and his codefendants had been "kidnapped" by train to Boise in 1906. Plans for the return train were premature. Haywood was free, but Moyer and Pettibone were yet to be tried. When their cases were dismissed, the original heat of triumph had cooled. No special arrangements were needed for Harry Orchard. He went to prison in a hack. He remained there the rest of his life. He may have visited the Idanha once more to deliver strawberries or chickens — he became an expert grower of both. It is known that he did get downtown ocassionally, under guard and anonymous, but a stop at the Idanha, the site of his original little black bag, is only interesting speculation.

As to the plea of guilty and his subsequent imprisonment, Orchard wrote in his book, *The Man God Made Again:*

"When the time came I insisted on pleading guilty, even against the advice of friends. . . . The judge asked me if I knew that such a course carried only the death penalty. I answered that I did. I was ready and willing to pay the penalty. I did not ask to have the sentence set aside. On the contrary, I wrote Charley Steunenberg and Governor Gooding to insist that the death sentence be carried out.

"When I was advised that there was a movement on foot to get my sentence commuted to life imprisonment my whole being revolted against this at first. But I was determined to do God's will. Jesus has never failed me since I have gone over to His side. But I came to the conclusion that I would leave the matter of life imprisonment in His hands. Then I had peace.

"I thank my friends who have stood by me so loyally and do not feel the least tinge of bitterness toward those who have opposed me. The Lord has taken all that out of my heart. The thing is settled with me now. I am happy I can face the future with courage and hope, by God's help endeavoring to live each day nearer to my God. . . . I hope I will not be charged with writing this to draw sympathy. Such a thought is furthest from my mind. I am writing this for the glory of God. If it were not for Him this old world would never have known of the awful life confessed to by Harry Orchard."

The confessed dynamiter became a cooperative prisoner. He made furniture for his cottage and for the children of numerous wardens. He grew chickens and turkeys, supervising the poultry operations that helped the prison with its food bill. He grew strawberries and other fruit.

Beaming of countenance, ruddy of complexion because he spent much time in the sun, he appeared sincere in his religious conviction when he gave occasional interviews. Orchard did not argue with visitors doubtful of his repentance. He merely smiled and said he was a new man. He changed the subject if the point was pressed.

Stewart H. Holbrook, author of a couple of books about Orchard's crimes, approached an interview with deep doubts. With permission of Warden Pearl Meredith he spent about an hour with Orchard in the early 1940s. He did not get much new, but he felt that Orchard expressed himself with evangelistic conviction. Holbrook, a rough-and-ready writer, ex-logger, and confidant of skid-row bums, said Orchard was either a superb actor or a dedicated Christian. He felt so strongly about the matter that he bought one of Orchard's books — which is not common for a reporter.

An incident that startled Holbrook almost as much as the audience with Orchard happened at dinner in the warden's house. The first course was a delicious soup, proclaimed by Holbrook and Dick d'Easum, then a reporter for *The Statesman* and serving as guide to Holbrook, as among the best they had ever had. Not only was the soup excellent but the lady who served it was a regular doll — hair like Clara Bow, sparkle in her eyes, and swinging hips to be envied by Marilyn Monroe.

"Who," asked Holbrook, "is this jewel of a maid?"

"Lyda Southard," said Warden Meredith. "She serves some great dishes."

Suddenly the soup did not seem so special. Lyda Southard, the notorious female Bluebeard, was doing a long stretch for killing a husband. Evidence at the trial indicated she had done away with three or four other husbands, poisoning them with the residue of flypaper dispensed in soup. Holbrook did not enjoy the rest of his meal. With slight urging from his guide he presently consumed a sandwich at the Idanha, where he was reasonably sure George Cordes, proprietor of the cafe, would permit no nonsense with flypaper.

As evidence to support Orchard's repentance, it is noteworthy that he was baptized in January 1909 in the big plunge bath at the prison. He expressed allegiance to the Seventh Day Adventists. For leading him to the light he thanked Julian Steunenberg, Mrs. Steunenberg, Dr. J. E. Froom, L. E. Froom who collaborated on his life story, Dean Hinks, and others.

Orchard died in April 1954. He was eighty-eight. He had been in prison forty-eight years and was one of the last of the participants in the noted trial. He was buried in Morris Hill Cemetery through influence of members of the Steunenberg family. The bronze marker reads: Harry Orchard. 1866–1954. "The Man God Made Again."

The IDAN-HA

The summer of 1907 is remembered by fans as the time Walter Johnson burned up the semipro baseball league of western Idaho. His pitching on various diamonds was fantastic. What he did at the Idanha was almost as surprising. Johnson and his Weiser Kids came to Boise for a doubleheader on the Fourth of July weekend. As usual, the team stayed at the Idanha. At midmorning, skies were dark. Rain threatened. A few drops fell. Expecting the game would be cancelled, Johnson wanted a workout to prevent loss of zip in his arm. No spot outdoors appealed, so he warmed up in the hotel hall, second floor. Guy Meats, the catcher who handled him in Weiser and went with him to the Washington Senators, squatted at the other end. Lacking a home plate to measure accuracy, Meats fetched a thundermug from his room. Johnson blazed a few fast ones over the crockery. Then, according to a yarn that has come down the ages as the real McCoy, he let one slip and smashed the pot. It was not surprising, since Johnson could toss a ball 100 miles per hour. Remnants of the pot were not saved, which is too bad for collectors of historic artifacts.

With orthodox equipment at his disposal, Johnson went out to clobber Boise that afternoon, as the rain gave way to almost clear skies. Johnson set records throughout the summer. The major one was seventy-four innings without allowing a score. He went to work for the Senators that fall, won a game early, and continued to pitch for many years. He won a fabulous number of major league games, including one in a World Series. He was made a member of the Baseball Hall of Fame.

Veteran baseball fans and advocates of the Idanha hotel's role claim that if it had not been for his workout in the hall he might have lost his skill, broken the string of victories, and never done his great deeds for the baseball world.

Baseball in the boondocks during the 1907 season was a game of flying spikes and dirty tricks. The Mountain Home team also put up at the Idanha, because a forty-mile trip was an excursion. Trains were not favorably scheduled. Autos were rare. Mountain Home had a pitcher rated next to Johnson in the league. Boise was worried because he was so overpowering. The weekend game late in the season was crucial, and Johnson had already gone to the majors, but Weiser was on top of the league. Mountain home and Boise were battling for second and for pride. The rivalry was keen.

On the morning of the big game the Mountain Home pitcher and one of his fielders, who was a heavy hitter, were arrested for rape. The alleged crime had occurred in Ada County. The baseball players insisted they were innocent. They were determined to appeal before a magistrate, have the matter quashed, or at least postponed until Monday.

Magistrates were either out of town or unwilling to tackle the sordid matter. Pitcher and fielder were taken into custody. Neither took part in the game. By a quirk of justice, Boise lost in spite of the blow to Mountain Home.

It turned out that the charges were engineered by the management of the Boise team. Names and all fit a pattern. The accused did know the girls. They were quite friendly. At least one of the alleged rapists was on the outs with his girl's mother, who wouldn't let him on the premises. The course of love had not been running smoothly. Criminal charges

Idaho Historical Society

Walter Johnson, pitcher for Weiser in 1907 and for many years a star in the majors, warmed up in the Idanha with astonishing results.

opened a doorway to respectable romance. When the defendants went to court they confronted their young ladies and assorted parents. The boys pled not guilty but expressed devotion to the girls. Would they marry the young ladies? You bet they would. They had been ready, willing, and eager for some time. So the next doubleheader the pitcher and fielder took part in was a double wedding. Villains of the Boise baseball team were not invited.

The IDAN-HA

William E. Borah had an extremely busy and anxious summer. At the top of his agenda, of course, was prosecuting the Haywood charges. Throughout the long trial, however, he was haunted by an indictment brought against him by a federal grand jury in March. The charge was timber fraud. Borah was attorney for officers of the Barber Lumber Company, forerunner of Boise Cascade. The government said the company had set up dummy purchasers of federal timber, paying a small amount to individuals who filed on the tracts and then taking over the land for logging by Barber Lumber. Borah was involved because he was said to have advised the officers that the transactions were lawful.

One of those named as a company stockholder and timber buyer in cahoots with Barber was Frank Steunenberg, the late governor whose assassination was the immediate cause of Borah's court activity in Boise. Steunenberg could not be brought to court, but the link to the Haywood case caused a great deal of rumor and speculation. Suggestions were whispered — and even shouted — that a faction was out to "get" Borah because of his vigorous part in the labor case.

In his book, *Borah of Idaho*, published in 1936 by Longmans, Green and Company, Claudius Johnson says there is no truth to that story.

"Darrow did tell Borah later that the Haywood defense felt some satisfaction after the indictment," Johnson wrote, "for it had reason to think such a charge would embarrass the Senator in his prosecution of Haywood. He was the only member of the prosecution who did not break down in the course of the trial."

The book goes on the say that Borah's indictment was directed by leading Idaho Republicans who were unhappy that Borah had been elected to the U.S. Senate by the Idaho Legislature. Jealousy was the root.

The land-fraud trial was set for summer. Partly because of motions filed by defendants other than Borah and partly because of Borah's chore in Boise, the case was postponed. When it did come before the bench in the fall of 1907, Senator Borah was defended by James Hawley. Another Boise lawyer, S. L. Tipton, also worked on the case for Borah.

Nearly all the time at the trial was spent by the government. Many witnesses were called. They told their stories of taking out claims to timberland that may or may not have been taken over by the lumber company. Hawley seldom interrupted or cross-questioned. He let the prosecution roll. At one point the judge asked Hawley if he were not uncommonly indifferent. Hawley replied that he was satisfied the testimony was doing his client no harm.

"Do you intend to call many witnesses?" asked the court.

"Only one, Your Honor," said Hawley. "Senator Borah will answer a few questions."

Borah was on the stand about twenty minutes. The government and defendant summed up. Hawley gave an unusually short summary. Within fifteen minutes after the judge read his instructions, the jury was back with a verdict of not guilty.

The night he was acquitted, there was a "monster" celebration at the Idanha. It was in the nature of a doubleheader for Borah and Hawley. The Columbia band led a parade to the Idanha. Borah and Hawley addressed a cheering crowd from the second-floor balcony.

"A monstrous wrong was done the senator," Hawley said.

"The prosecution was an attempt to prevent the course of justice and to gratify the personal hatred of those who had it in charge."

Borah was given a tremendous ovation, a news story said. "The tumult continued for some time before the senator could hear his own voice."

"I cannot express to you my appreciation of your confidence," he said. "I would rather go to jail with the love and loyalty of such friends as a consolation than to be acquitted and have your distrust. It would seem I was indicted and tried because I was a warm friend of ex-governor Steunenberg. There is a certain species of human hyenas who find no gratification in fighting the living, but fatten upon the dead."

Main Street was crowed from Sixth to Tenth. Traffic was suspended at the Idanha corner. The celebration continued with fireworks and torpedoes. Borah was picked up and carried into the hotel on the shoulders of admirers. He again spoke from the balcony. The hotel lobby and street were filled for more than a hour after his final words of appreciation.

Borah had another inning during the spring of 1908. President Roosevelt fired N. M. Ruick, the district attorney who had prosecuted the senator. Teddy passed the word to his attorney general. The gentlemen, General Bonaparte, delegated the job to A. W. Cooley, an assistant attorney general, who came to Boise to announce the dismissal. The President also fired Marshal Ruel Rounds. Senator Borah had the privilege of naming the successors. He agreed to the interim appointment of Miles Johnson as attorney for Idaho. He nominated Shad L. Hodgin, sheriff of Ada County, to be U.S. marshal. His nominations were confirmed.

Cooley made a statement explaining the removal of Ruick. "For some time past," he said, "his attitude in connection with certain departmental matters of more than ordinary importance has been utterly inconsistent with the idea of proper loyalty to the government."

The indictment of Borah was specified in a letter to Ruick from another official as the cause of his dismissal. "There was serious public dissatisfaction," the letter said. "You showed excessive urgency before the grand jury."

Idaho Historical Society

Senator William E. Borah addressed a crowd of admirers from the Idanha balcony in 1907 when he was found not guilty in a land-fraud trial.

The IDAN-HA

A woman of mystery stirred Boise's curiosity in the spring of 1908. Her visit became the sensation of the social season. She registered at the Idanha as Mrs. Henry Norton of New York. The best rooms had been reserved for her. She made it clear to the clerk that she was not to be disturbed.

Her stay at the hotel might have gone unobserved except that it was unusual for a lady to be traveling with a colored butler and her personal attorney. Furthermore, Mrs. Norton has such aristocratic bearing she seemed to be someone other than a commoner.

The Statesman revealed the facts after prying deep and exercising its best detective talents. The day after Mrs. Norton arrived, the paper unmasked her as Madame Lilian Nordica, America's foremost operatic soprano. Confronted by the evidence, the lady was angry at first and then friendly. She agreed to an interview in her suite. The reporter was probably Mrs. Eva Hunt Dockery, although there is no byline.

"You may think me rather insistant," the reporter said.

"Yes, I do," said Madame Nordica.

Then, the story went on, Madame Nordica leaned forward and "in the most captivating manner and with all the interest of a small child said: 'Well, I didn't intend to let it leak out but I will tell you a secret. I am here to see the Sells-Floto Circus on Monday."

Passing up that alibi for the moment, the reporter — surely a woman — said that the visitor had beautiful auburn hair. The gushy paragraph then said the madame (always with the "e") was wearing a charming negligee of white Pompadour silk brocaded in bunches of pink roses. She was described as a home-loving matron who delighted in making some of her own clothes. She stitched on something during the interview.

Male reporters, who looked at the story from another angle, thought Madame Nordica was gifted at sewing, all right, but that her specialty was embroidery. Here to attend the circus? What rot. She had circuses all over her native Maine and an abundance in Boston and New York where she lived most of the time. It must have been something other than elephants and tigers that brought her to Idaho. The fact that Sells-Floto was showing in Boise, they speculated, was a handy coincidence. Unless she was fixing to sign up with the circus as a barker, her story was as full of holes as a punchboard.

Why, actually, was the operatic singer in Boise? Well, she was going to Idaho City to settle a mining claim. She was interested in taking out a homestead at the Twin Falls land opening. She was a potential investor in Boise real estate. The list of possibilities was long. To each suggestion Madame Nordica put on the face of a sphinx and smiled. She admitted nothing.

What she did do was take a long carriage ride around Boise with her Negro servant as footman and her attorney in a following vehicle. She said she liked Boise. The scenery was impressive, the Natatorium remarkable. Following the ride she took lunch in her room. All meals, during her stay of several days, were brought up from the Idanha kitchen.

Members of the Idanha staff were angry that the visitor had been identified and disturbed. Before her arrival the entire crew, from floor moppers to top management, had promised not to breathe a word. Madame's secrecy was to be preserved not only during her stay but after she had gone. Nobody knew who spilled the beans.

Reporters who turned from the singer to her attorney found him just as evasive. How about the rumor that she was getting a divorce? No answer.

"Madame is on her way to the West Coast to meet a singing engagement," he said. "She has finished a season of performances in Washington, D.C., and has come west for fun." The trip to Idaho, he said, was a respite from her endeavors to build a college on the Hudson.

Her interest in circuses was enhanced during her second day when she visited a Sells-Floto auditor in his railway car when she learned he was ill. No particular friendship, she said. She just admired circus people and liked to cheer them up.

The noted diva expanded her enthusiasm for Sells-Floto by going to an afternoon performance. A clown met her at the gate and led her to a reserved seat. She was wearing a queenly velvet robe and a circlet of jewels on her auburn hair. As she marched to her fir-plank throne she paused to greet a child. The tot reached out a hand. She took it and cooed to the infant in baby talk. The circus band played a salute.

Madame Nordica departed without saying more about why she came. Perhaps it was to see the circus. Maybe she was going to buy a summer home on Payette Lakes. The gossip of divorce continued among the teacups. She took the train for San Francisco. The mystery of her Boise visit remains a mystery. Idanha Hotel workers weren't saying, if they knew. Today there is no one to ask.

The Nordica story was complicated by confusing Mr. Arthur McGhee, the singer's attorney, with James McGee, a Boise resident who was shot at by his wife during the time the soprano was in town. Vocal organs being what they are and ears being quick to pick up a juicy report, the story was batted about that Mr. McGhee had been drilled by a

Sells-Floto worker. That was far from the truth. The lawyer was neither drilled nor did he drill anybody.

It was a Mrs. James McGee who caused the hubbub. It seems she took a pop or two at her husband outside a saloon on Main Street. She missed him several times but bagged a buggy hitched near the saloon. Fortunately, the shots also missed the horses. Where Mr. McGee ducked at the time was not clear. One minute he was near the buggy, the next he was invisible.

Prosecutor Koelsch investigated. On the basis of evidence given him by officers who disarmed the lady, he felt some sort of crime had been committed. When Mr. McGee was found, he declined to file charges against his wife. He said there had been a difference of opinion and that she might have tried to follow him to the saloon on Main Street, about a block from the Idanha. As to the shooting, he said he had heard shots but didn't know why they were fired or at what.

An early letterhead with a picture of the hotel

Because he was unable to find a statute defining assault on a buggy with a firearm, the county attorney charged Mrs. McGee with disturbing the peace. She admitted that, and paid a fine. Peace was restored to the corner.

Citizens who wanted to avoid degrading brawls at bars quenched their thirst at the Idanha Pharmacy, which in 1907 boasted the finest soda fountain in the city. The ad praised "drinks made the Idanha way." Specials were Mexican lime freeze with imported limes, Idanha grape cooler, We We sundae, and Emerald sundae.

The spring of 1908 was also the time of the Little Eva scam. A gypsy maid shuttled around the hotel circuit, begging meals and money. Because she was deaf she conducted her business with signs and notepad. Some benefactors complained that they missed watches and cash after they had met the young lady. Little Eva was marched off to police court. She denied any wrong, writing note after note to explain that she was a poor, deaf Gypsy lass. Sympathy of a curious crowd was all in favor of Eva until Officer Claus Peterson spoke to her in Swedish. Little Eva responded with Scandanavian oration denouncing police and their ancestors. That did her in. It turned out that she was not deaf, was not a Gypsy, but was a Swedish transient making a fair living. She had been Little Eva only a short time. At her previous stand on the Pacific Coast she had been Mona DeMarie. For a few days she was prisoner Greta, still swearing in Swedish.

Hotels in general suffered a blemish that season. Doings at the notorious Hoffman House on Eighth Street raised eyebrows of the fastidious, as well as knobs on the craniums of Hoffman customers. A bartender conked another bartender on the skull with the barrel of a revolver. Apparently the bartender of the first part found the bartender of the second part in bed with a woman who had once been chummy with bartender No. 1 but who at the time of the altercation had moved to the Hoffman House from Levy's alley.

The pistol-whipper told officers he didn't care much

what the woman or her current lover did, but they were making a great deal too much racket in their room, carrying on in loud shouts and breaking furniture. He was afraid the commotion might disturb other guests.

The solution was banishment from Boise for all three. *The Statesman* added that the "foul resort" should be abated. It was closed for a time, resumed business on a shoestring, and eventually succumbed to the wrecking ball.

One of Boise's most shocking events of 1907, year of more than average shock in several categories, was the sudden death in July of Peter Sonna, a prominent citizen who had taken a notable role in starting the Idanha. He owned several business properties, the most familiar being the Sonna Building with its opera house. He was vice president of the First National Bank and an officer of the Artesian Hot and Cold Water Company. He served as Boise's mayor in 1893.

He had bought the Idanha corner from the Presbyterian church when the church decided to move from the business center. He sold to the Idanha company because he wanted Boise to have a good hotel. He was a long-time friend of the McMillans and their associates on the board of directors.

Another event, primarily of interest to the hotel fraternity, was the retirement of Frank Blackinger as manager of the Capital Hotel, late in July. The veteran innkeeper from Silver City had managed the Capital for eight years. His successor was Otto Kline. The new owner was the Idaho Brewing Company. Blackinger's retirement was by no means final. He was in and out of the Capital in one capacity or another, and he worked for other hotels and lounges in Boise. He was respected as a source of historical wit and wisdom long after he finally did retire to his home on Franklin Street.

An unusual visitor at the Idanha that summer was W. S. Grayson, a Pony Express rider in the 1860s. It was not the fact that he had carried mail pouches in that exciting era that made him unusual. He had come West to find his grave and had found it somewhere in Utah. He was pleased to report to pals in Boise that the mistake was verified. What had happened, he said, was that one day during a close race with Indians he had lost his hat. Another man was killed and, because of the hat, was identified as Grayson. For many years, he said, he had been trying to find out where he was buried. It was more that a little bothersome, he said, to put a flower on his own tomb.

Hotel management was up to its ears in difficulty that summer. Telephone girls went on strike. All the Myrts and Mables in the state quit asking "Number please?" They wanted more money and shorter hours. The Idanha had its enunciator, linking rooms with the desk, but that was no help in getting outside numbers. Executives manned the switchboard for a few days. They were in a state of anxiety, though, because telephone girls at Lewiston had beaten up their manager. It was not at all restful to man the cords, the hotel people said, when at any minute you might be bashed with an umbrella. Arbitration prevailed after a week or so. The hello girls gained a point or two. Service was restored.

Boise Hotels were not out of the woods with respect to woman trouble. In 1908, nearly three-quarters of a century before ERA flexed its mouth and muscle, maids, waitresses, and other females at the Idanha joined their sisters in several businesses in demanding escorts home after dark. They said there was an epidemic of attacks on young girls. It wasn't safe to walk the streets. Their wages did not allow cabs. Facts about assaults were vague. There was said to be a purse snatcher, or worse, down by the railway station. Perhaps there was a gang that preyed on working maidens. A strange man with a wicked glint in his alcoholic eye was rumored to have insulted a girl when she got off a streetcar near the Nat.

The Idanha met the crisis boldly. It assigned men from its staff, plus some recruits willing to accept the challenge, to guard the girls on their nocturnal journeys. That squelched the complaint faster than you can say moonlight and roses. After only a couple of nights some of the ladies asked that their escorts be dismissed because the gents were more demanding than the unknown attackers. Others found their company so pleasant that they married them. Fear of violence to gentle creatures was conquered by more noble passions.

The IDAN-HA

From the day it opened it 1901, the Idanha had transportation for its guests from railway station to hotel door. The carriage met all trains at the Front Street platform. The trip was free for patrons with reservations and for regular drummers. Unscheduled guests paid a small fee that could be charged to the room or overlooked if the cab driver was adequately tipped. Horse carriages were the chief mode of transportation until about 1910, when the auto became top dog.

A sparkplug in the early success of the auto was a trip from Philadelphia to Seattle in 1909. Idaho had a share in the adventure. So did the Idanha in a minor way.

The trip was sponsored by Harry Kingston of the *Philadelphia Press* to demonstrate the need for a national turnpike. Relays of different cars and drivers were to carry a message from President Taft to the president of the Alaska-Yukon-Pacific Exposition. The first car roared away from the newspaper office in Philadelphia late in September. It went about a quarter of a mile. It smashed into a pole, killing the first messenger. For a time it seemed the trip was cancelled. Then the sponsor decided to try again. He lined up drivers across the country. A tentative time schedule was drawn up, along with the route and potential relay points. Another car and another team chugged out of Philadelphia on the second attempt. Things went smoothly. President Taft, however, elected to go to Seattle by train. He had a date to keep at the exposition and didn't want to be changing a tire in Nebraska or some such place.

Cars taking off on the second round had better luck than the first. At least nobody was killed. Blown tires and sputtering engines caused exasperating delays, but the show went on. Early in October the team reached Idaho at Soda Springs and hurried on to Arco. There a fresh auto and crew took over. Harry Wilson's thirty-horse-power Mitchell bounced away in a cloud of dust for Hailey, with Calvin Story as chauffeur and Emmett Russell as assistant driver — riding shotgun and as it turned out in a more literal sense than might be expected. T. E. Picotte, editor of the *Wood River Times,* went along as publicity agent. The road was terrible. Somewhere between the Craters of the Moon and Silver Creek the outfit managed to get lost. One rut was much like another. First thing they knew they were out of road and just about out of ruts. To pass the time profitably while they figured a way out of the brush, they shot sage grouse. Russell, with his shotgun, got in splendid licks. Birds were plentiful. Editor Picotte was happy to report when the car finally pulled into Hailey that they had enough birds for a chamber of commerce dinner at the Hiawatha.

The relay car could not wait for birds or oratory. The roadster buzzed away across Camas Prairie to Soldier.

Two Boise drivers went to Soldier to handle the next leg. L. J. Duel and C. H. Coffin, described as a couple of the most skillful auto jockeys in the city, drove L. L. Ormsby's Buick. They had a breeze. The journey was so smooth the drivers whizzed back the next day, arriving in Boise October 3.

The men who had just done their bit had a sort of press conference with the next driver over coffee and sandwiches at the Idanha, a handy oasis not far from the garage that serviced cars. Partisans of the Buick urged that Ormby's auto be driven on the next leg. Nathan Alexander insisted on using his Thomas Flyer, and he did. He made it to Weiser in about four hours, which was fantastic.

Fay Lloyd of Weiser was scheduled to drive to Baker but was unable to accept the assignment. A substitute filled the bill. Oregon drivers handled the relay to the Washington border above Portland.

From Philadelphia to Seattle the relay took about twelve days, not including the time lost by the opening disaster at the Philadelphia city limits. The time was gratifying to the sponsors, who had a hard time explaining that the trip was not a race. There was no competition except the calendar. The intent was to call attention to the need for better roads and to advertise the Seattle exposition. The written message carried by the drivers from President Taft to the fair hardly justified two weeks of effort, the use of a dozen cars, and the strain of several dozen blown tires. It said in substance: "Congratulations to the Alaska-Yukon Pacific Exposition." Taft had, in fact, personally said as much several days earlier when he appeared on the same stand to which the final automobile delivered his letter.

Idaho had more of the exposition to think about than its part in the relay. It was exceedingly angry with the whole shebang. The occasion became known as the case of the hot salted peanut. The fuss brought two sister states as close to the brink of breaking off diplomatic relations as anything since the Civil War. The squabble merits attention here, although it had little or nothing to do with the Idanha Hotel. Well, Governor James Brady did stay at the Idanha a short time before he took a residence on Main Street. That's the umbilical cord. The battle at the Seattle fair is worth reviewing in any case.

Idaho eagerly accepted the invitation to provide an exhibit of its best products. Governor Brady and his fair commissioner, A. D. McKinley, asked for a delay in filling its space because the June opening was no time for prime agricultural crops. That concession was made by Seattle.

Idaho sent over carloads of minerals, pictures of breathtaking scenery, and samples of handiwork by school children. Further exhibits were to be displayed as prize produce ripened. Idaho was permitted to occupy additional space, mostly because H. F. Samuels of Wallace, superintendent of the mining section, wanted to show almost one hundred thousand pounds of minerals. One rock weighed fifteen tons, another ten tons. A space adjoining Idaho's original building was granted. A gubernatorial party geared up in Boise for ruffles and flourishes. Governor Brady chose a retinue composed of colonels, Attorney General D. C. McDougall, and Secretary of State Robert Lansdon. Military men in the unit were outfitted with special uniforms with enough gold braid to impress Buckingham Palace.

The day the delegation was to embark by train, the governor got a telegram from Seattle. It read: "Have been arrested for trying to stop management from putting a peanut booth in front of the building on our grounds. What position shall I take? Signed A. D. McKinley, Idaho commissioner."

Hot on the heels of that came another from I. A. Nadeau, director general of the commission. It said: "Some trouble occurred today between Commissioner McKinley and one of our departments. You may be sure the matter will be straightened out."

Governor Brady did not rest assured. He did not rest at all. He boiled. He telegraphed to Commissioner McKinley: "Think your action all right. We do not want cheap booth in front of our building. Wire me fully what action has been taken by management. May conclude not to proceed beyond Portland if disrespect has been shown the state by treatment of you."

To Director General Nadeau he wired: "I approve Commissioner McKinley's action. I doubt it will be well for us to go beyond Portland unless the matter is satisfactorily explained. I leave on train No. 11 this evening and will expect answer at once."

More messages exchanged during the day shed light on the squabble. The trouble had started when a crew of laborers excavated sod from a patch of ground in front of the Idaho building. McKinley took it in stride until carpenters started laying log walls. He said that would not do at all. He would not stand for a shack at that spot, squarely in the line of traffic to the Idaho exhibit. When he was informed that the edifice under construction was a peanut stand, he blew his top. He ordered the crew to quit. A laborer, apparently the foreman, menaced McKinley with a shovel. Unyielding, the commissioner turned his indignation up a few notches. "If you hit me," he said, "you are hitting the state of Idaho." The workman put down his shovel and hastened to higher authority.

Next thing McKinley knew he was arrested and tossed off the exhibition grounds. Guards let him linger at the gate long enough to surrender his pass. Then he was cast into outer darkness, with no prospect of returning to his duties. The Idaho display was not finished. The governor was even then packing his portfolio and writing his speech of appreciation. The fat, in short, was in the fire.

Resourceful in the face of adversity, McKinley smuggled a message to the California booth. The commissioner of that state sneaked to the fence to chat with the outcast. California advised Idaho to stand its ground. The California gentleman said he had run into similar trouble with his concession resulting in pip-squeak vendors hogging his space. So had Oregon. California said he would take the dispute to the big boss. He left McKinley gazing wistfully on the promised land through a woven wire fence.

Back in Boise, Governor Brady paced his office. "I feel we have one of the most artistic buildings on the grounds," he told reporters. "We do not propose to have any peanut stands or any cheap outfits occupying any of our space. I fully approve of Commissioner McKinley's action. I cannot help feeling his arrest was caused by some unauthorized subordinate. The management has treated us royally. However, if upon investigation I find this action is approved by the management, I feel if would be improper for myself and staff to participate in the opening exercises."

A short time after he delivered that warning he had the word he was hoping for: "President Chilberg has rescinded my arrest and ordered the booth removed. Signed, McKinley."

Peanuts, zero; potatoes, yippee.

Governor Brady accepted the apology. Washington and Idaho shook hands. Peace and harmony again prevailed. The peanut stand was demolished.

Resplendent in uniforms decorated with gold lace, the Idaho party escorted Governor Brady in top hat and tails to the battleship Tennessee and the flagship of the Japanese navy. Under the direction of a Japanese admiral the battleship fired a salute to His Excellency. The din smothered toots of all the peanut stands in King County.

That was the end of the peanut altercation. Idaho was further pleased with Washington for another event. Much to the enrichment of conversation at the Idanha, where many people still thought constantly of the Orchard case, William D. Haywood was brought to justice in Yakima. The man who had beat a charge of conspiracy to murder a governor was hauled up on a charge of smoking a cigaret in a forbidden zone. He admitted guilt and paid a fine of $2.50 plus $5.45 costs.

The IDAN-HA

A business conference at the Idanha launched one of Boise's most popular amusement spots. G. W. Hull, who knew a thing or two about carnivals and dance halls, sought the advice of several business leaders about having a center where young and old could kick up their heels, giggle at odd images, and buy tons of popcorn. The suggestion resulted in White City Park, next to the Natatorium on the East end of Warm Springs Avenue. The Nat and the amusement park were so close they were parts of the same setup. For many years White City Park was famous for its hall of mirrors, scenic railway, and Fighting Bob.

G. W. Hull's first name was Gladden. It fit. He did a great deal to gladden the hearts of young people. Nothing gladdened the spirits of kids as much as Fighting Bob. He was a tough old ostrich. Hull got him in California to give variety to his layout, which included just about everything calculated to entertain people who like roller skating, dancing, kewpie doll stands, grip testers, ice cream cones, and roller coasters.

Fighting Bob was named for Bob Fitzsimmons, the heavyweight boxer. The ostrich was a heavyweight for his kind. He could fight like a champion, too.

Manager Hull had only a transient connection with the Idanha, moving to White City Park as soon as it took shape. However, it is believed that he wanted to strut Fighting Bob to the Idanha from the railway station where he was unloaded, and then up Main to the amusement park. The plan fell apart, along with the ostrich crate, when Fighting Bob threw a fit. He objected to the entire deal. He didn't like cages and ropes. He didn't like people. He didn't like Boise. So Hull had him taken to the park in a covered box aboard a dray. It was a tame beginning for a wild career.

As soon as Boise boys learned the ostrich struck with beak and feet, they teased him so much he was dangerous to the unsuspecting. Ladies from the country would be strolling by the fence saying nice things about ostriches when Bob would smack them a vigorous blow. He applauded himself with hissing and cackling.

His appetite was tremendous. He ate anything. Boys delighted in feeding him chewing tobacco, gum, marshmallows, golf balls, and cigar butts. The assorted menu didn't seem to hurt him. He was just as healthy after a lunch of junk as he was when he had his prepared mash and vegetables.

If Fighting Bob had not been such a willing garbage can and such a two-footed fighter he probably would not have taken first billing from the scenic railway. For the sake of arms, legs, and clothing it is just as well he did detain young people from the roller coaster. It was a thriller, reaching what seemed to be about half a mile into the sky and winding its breathtaking course around scary turns on wooden pilings that often vibrated as though they were coming apart. The most fun for many boys who rode the coaster were the breakdowns, which happened several times a day. There you were, leaning over a seat almost on eye level with Table Rock, waving at mortals below, hoping somebody would recognize you and worry whether you would fall off and break your neck or get down in time for dinner. Hull was generous about the roller coaster. He gave the dime back if there was a mechanical delay. He could have charged a quarter for those trips; they were more fun.

White City Park got a mate for Fighting Bob. Hull got the hen ostrich from the same place he got Bob. The day she arrived there was another celebration downtown, including the Idanha of course. Hull announced at a Commercial Club luncheon that there would soon be eggs and eventually little ostriches all over the park.

No eggs were laid. A veterinarian gave the answer. Fighting Bob's mate was another male. G. W. Hull was not elated. There is a report, not verified, of the remarks that passed between him and the ostrich agent:

"You got stuck," said the ostrich seller.

"Guaranteed," said Hull.

"I'll guarantee you something else, mister," said the agent. "I'll guarantee if you get any ostrich eggs you will lay them yourself."

The park bought another mate, being sure to get a hen. She was Desdemona, and she did lay eggs. Hardly any hatched. The chicks that did hatch soon died. Fighting Bob grew more cantankerous than ever. Baiting him became a leading recreation. One night about 1919 a bunch of teenagers tried to ride him. They got a rope around his beak and a sort of cinch around his body. One of the more adventurous boys leaped aboard. Fighting Bob did a couple of crowhops and sailed clean over the ten-foot, woven-wire fence. Witnesses swore he flew. Once over the fence he stretched his long legs in a gallop for Boise River. Only by clinging to the rope around his body did the buckaroo keep him from swimming the river. The rider, naturally, was afoot by that time and hollering for help.

They got Fighting Bob back into the pen. That was the last time he was tormented.

The ostrich pined for a while but lived a couple of years longer. Although threatened at one time with pneumonia, it was a fit of anger that killed Fighting Bob. He struck at something, and his claw ripped a frightful gash in his throat. He died in a few minutes.

Stuffed and still defiant of eye, Fighting Bob stands

today in a glass case in the office of Boise's zoo. With him are several ostrich eggs which may have been produced by Desdemona. For many years before he was moved to the zoo, the mounted Fighting Bob was in the Idaho museum in the statehouse.

The IDAN-HA

Several men were managers of the Idanha. Some did a couple of hitches. After the resignation of John Cage in 1901, within a year of the hotel's opening, the directors appointed E. W. Schubert, who had had experience at the Overland. He served until 1908 but by no means disappeared from the hotel scene.

Then came Charles Grout, a whiz-bang backslapper, yarn spinner, cuisine artist, and champion greeter. Another part of this book will relate some of his activities. He was manager from 1908 to 1913.

To succeed Grout the hotel board chose Ray F. VanSlyke. He began his duties in January 1917. In September he was dismissed. Robert Aikman, a director, became acting manager. He had too many other businesses to permit necessary attention to the hotel, so early in 1915 he dropped the reins and J. V. Sweetman was hired. Sweetman separated from the company in the fall of 1917, and Silas Peake was employed as chief clerk and acting manager. In June 1918 Peake went out, and Sweetman was returned to the front desk as clerk and manager. Early in his second tour the Idanha had two important developments. The barber shop in the basement was leased to B. McElroy and A. L. Jones. The dining room and cafe, operated from the start by the hotel, were leased to H. L. Thompson. In March 1920 the dining facilities were leased to George Cordes on a ten-year contract that he renewed in 1930.

Leslie Pearson was chief clerk and acting manager for several years in the 1920s. In 1926, when Thomas McMillan had taken over as general manager, Jennie Gates was honored for twenty years of service in various capacities. On that occasion veteran members of the staff recalled that Mabel Tracy, an assistant clerk in 1910, had been elected Boise Princess for the Fourth of July celebration. For twenty-five years after that she traveled much of the West with her husband, Harry Tracy, a sporting goods salesman. After his death she married Carl Hipp. She died in February 1982 at the age of ninety-seven.

In 1929, with Thomas McMillan managing the operation, the Idanha remodeled the lobby and parlor. Meier and Frank of Portland did the job for about $2,400. Several bathrooms were added upstairs. At the same time the hotel company sold lots north of the building, fronting on Tenth and Bannock. The property has since been the site of several businesses.

Andrew Little of Emmett became a director in the fall of 1930. Hazel Morrow (later Mrs. Harry Shellworth) also became a director. Her father, J. B. Morrow, was one of the original incorporators. At his death in 1909 his stock went to his widow, Viva Skiff Morrow, and through her estate to Hazel Morrow.

As an indicator of the regard livestock growers have for each other, the Idanha, founded by stockmen, loaned a substantial sum to the Robert Noble estate in 1925 for construction of an office building at Tenth and Main. The reason given in the minute book is that the building would benefit the hotel. Noble was a major stockman of Owyhee County. He had opened a generous purse to the Idanha when it was getting started.

Thomas McMillan was manager in fact for many years. Chief clerks and acting managers served with him, but he was the boss. During his last years his daughter, Mrs. Roxie Johnson, looked after many of the decisions and details. She managed the Idanha for fifteen years. Thomas McMillan died in 1952. Mrs. Johnson, wife of Ansgar Johnson, photographer, sold the hotel to the Broadbent Estate in 1962 for nearly three times what it cost in 1900.

Clarence Hemphill, formerly of the Owyhee, was chief clerk and assistant manager circa 1940. He retired from active work in hotel operation and other business some years ago. In 1982 he went to Florida to live with a son, Gen. John Hemphill. He died in 1983.

Jess Jennison managed the hotel while it was owned by the Broadbent interests, with Alice Tetrick as chief stimulator. Mrs. Tetrick was the wife of Art Tetrick, a legatee of the Broadbent interests. She proved to be a whirlwind at the hotel, effecting many physical changes.

The Owyhee was opened in 1910 by E. W. Schubert, a former manager of the Idanha. The Owyhee was owned many years by the Falk family.

Idaho Historical Society

She referred to herself as a furniture mover. She put zest into an establishment that had slumped because of motel popularity. Jennison was responsible for innovations and astute management that brought operations back into the mainstream. It was during his tenure that the Idanha was placed on the National Register of Historic Places.

Idaho Historical Society

The Idanha was placed in the National Register of Historic Places in 1976. Jess Jennison (right) then hotel manager, and Keith Gabriel, head of Boise's Bicentennial Commission, anchored the plaque.

In recent years the Idanha has been operated by Idanha Properties.

E. W. Schubert, manager from 1902 to 1908, kept his hand in the hotel business by organizing a company that built the Owyhee in 1910. He was the first proprietor, taking a great deal of satisfaction in providing stiff competition to the hotel that had let him go. There are indications that he had his eye on another hotel before the Owyhee developed. That was the Boise Hotel, proposed as early as 1907 by a group of potential investors. The site was in the vicinity of Eighth and Bannock. The promoters, including several of Boise's successful business and professional tycoons, collected a nest egg. Construction was delayed. The project hung fire until 1930, when Hotel Boise was built under new conditions and by a different corporation.

At his retirement from the Idanha, *The Statesman* had this to say about Schubert:

"He is one of the best known and most popular hotel men in the west. Under his management the Idanha has taken front rank among the hotels of the country and has done as much as any one thing to advertise Boise to the world. Mr. Schubert became identified with the Idanha in 1901 when it first opened, as assistant manager, and in the latter part of the year became manager, which position he has occupied until the present time. His resignation has been in the hands of the company for some time but it was only last week that his successor had been decided upon. The hotel has been enlarged and improved right along under his management and has been made a paying institution. Two years ago the European plan was adopted and a handsome cafe added, bringing the hotel right up to date with the eastern cities. It has proved a great success in every way.

"After his retirement Mr. Schubert will devote his attention to his private interests and to developing and colonizing the Boise and Payette valleys."

That forecast may have been valid at the time. By 1910 Schubert was more devoted to the problem of putting people in rooms of the Owyhee than getting settlers and irrigation for farmland.

Charles Grout, his successor, was gifted in nourishment. His talent from boyhood was the art of elegant eating. He could write menu cards in half a dozen languages. Elaborate concoctions to please the taste buds of the fastidious were his duck soup. Formidable combinations in French, Italian, and Russian rolled off his tongue like the alphabet. Correct wines to go with beef, goose, or whatnot were as familiar to his culinary senses as two times two was to a math teacher. In other words, he knew his groceries.

A scrapbook belonging to the Idanha tells a lot about his background. He was born in Schnectady, New York, in 1870. At the age of fourteen he was a newsboy at the United States Hotel in Saratoga. A few years later he was a clerk in the commissary department of the New York Central Railway. He advanced to assistant chef in the dining car service. From 1901 to 1908 he was superintendent of dining cars for the Oregon Short Line of the Union Pacific system, with headquarters at Ogden. On special occasions he had dreams of duplicating meals he learned about at the Saratoga. A menu spread at a contemporary inn, the Somerset, must have been a special favorite because he pasted the clipping in his scrapbook. Here it is:

Canape: caviar frais, huîtres, potage tortue vert clair, céleri, amandes, olives, sherry; poisson: éperlans dip-

President W. H. Taft (center) rode through Boise in a welcoming parade with Gov. James Hawley (right) and Senator W. E. Borah. The man at the far left is not identified.

Idaho Historical Society

Charles Grout was famous for his meals and his jovial greeting as hotel manager before World War One.

lomatique, concombres, sauterne; releve: bouchées de ris de veau, Somerset pommes, haricots verts; sorbet à la imperials, Nestor cigarettes; roti: canards sauvages ruddy, hominy frit, salade endive; entremets de douceur, Apollinaris; glace aux marrons en Bellevue, petits fours fantasie; fromage de Camembert, Roquefort, café noir, cigars.

That adds up to about eleven courses. Twelve, if you call coffee a course. Somewhere in all that high-falutin language there must be something to eat. Quite a lot to eat. Even if you were a common clod like Jiggs of the funny paper you could make out a snack. A very important citizen did at its unveiling. He not only tucked the courses away with relish but he knew his way through the thickets of language. The dinner was prepared for William Howard Taft, then secretary of war and later president of the United States. He was fond of good food, a trait that made him America's heaviest president. The fact that Taft was such a trencherman had influence on Grout. He became one of Boise's noted gourmets. He grew corpulent.

He earned a reputation for choice rations at the Idanha. Some menus which he whipped up for festive dates rival the repast for Secretary Taft. There had hardly been the like in Boise before and rarely since. Western style being what it is — and was then — even well-heeled citizens who could buy the restaurant were likely to bawl like branded calves if they were faced with a bill of fare in French in a dining room dimly lit with candles. Grout's grub turned many into connoisseurs.

Meals on dining cars in the West were better than brown baggers, but they could not come up to the standard of the plush resorts in New York. Grout did his best to match the fare with affordable prices. As commissary — that's the term on his business card — he spread a good table, at the same time keeping the management happy because he did not go overboard on snails and caviar.

An idea the commissary picked up from a New York restaurant did not fit railway dining cars. Grout saved it for the Idanha. The gimmick was a gift for the lucky customer. In the case of the New York restaurant it was a noble reward. On Saturday nights the proprietor selected a certain chair — known only to him and located on a card placed in the safe. The host alerted the cashier to watch the chair. When someone sat there, a ceremony broke out. Waiters with lighted candles marched to the spot with a silver tray on which reposed an inverted bowl. Beneath the bowl was a gold watch. It became a gift to the lucky diner.

Gold watches were a little steep for the Idanha. Grout worked the deal on a lesser scale, giving out tickets to the Pinney Theatre and passes to minstrel shows.

Five years after he took on the job of managing the hotel, a summary of his success was written for the *Salt Lake Tribune* by C. E. Arney:

"I remember a significant remark made by an oldtimer in 1900 at the corner of Tenth and Main when the little old church was being torn down to be supplanted by the Idanha hotel. He mused in this fashion:

"'John McMillan and his brother Tom, Bob Aikman and John Morrow will run many a band of sheep through that brick and lumber before they make it pay interest on their investment.'

"The conversationalist was not a pessimist or a knocker, but he belonged to that large army of individuals — well meaning but faulty in judgment — who are minus the courage to invade new fields of operation in the commercial world, which appears to be demanded by the public.

"These four men were early pioneers of Idaho who had waded through the hardships of personal inspection of their businesses on the range of the Gem of the Mountains. They had all passed through the experience of personal contact with the rather extreme vocation of sheep raising in the Rocky Mountains.

"They had lain out at nights on the ground with a saddle as their pillow and awoke in the morning to find their berth filled with water from a murky sky in their due protection of their flocks. This degree of protection had served to amass fortunes for each, which they aspired to invest in a business of remuneration to them and of appreciation to their neighbors and friends in the community of Boise where each had located and built comfortable if not spacious homes for themselves and their splendid families. This is the brief history of the beginning of Boise's first new hotel, the Idanha.

"For ten years it served as the undisputed center of commercial, political and social Boise. Ofttimes the International Irrigation Congress, for instance, extended its prestige as headquarters for the state and other government. This week the Idanha has completed its work of rebuilding and refitting the hotel on the familiar corner, and today it presents a cheerful, cleanly, and attractive appearance after a period of months of remodeling in which the proprietors have expended $30,000. Five thousand dollars has been spent for the lobby alone.

"The manager of this popular hostelry is Charles H. Grout, who has served more than five years in this capacity and who is well known in hotel and dining-car circles throughout the country."

A magazine of the hotel trade heaped compliments on the manager.

"Charles H. Grout is one of Idaho's best known and most popular hotel managers," it said. "His executive ability is perhaps best illustrated when it is made known that he has successfully conducted the New Idanha Hotel over a period of the very fiercest competition and against a corporation erecting another splendid hostelry in Boise. Charlie Grout is admittedly the most capable and one of the best liked Bonifaces in Boise. He is just about as well liked all over the intermountain country. Anyway, the traveling men swear by him.

"Today the New Idanha takes rank with any hotel of the first-rate class in the Pacific West. Its accommodations are of the very best that the traveling public could wish. The prices are in accord with traveling tastes, and everything that should be combined under the roof of the real hotel will be found at the New Idanha. Every attache under Mr. Grout must please the traveling public. And talk about cuisine! Charlie Grout's grill is the par excellence of anything between Salt Lake City and Portland. Twenty years ago Mr. Grout received his early training which so ably fitted him for his present work. . . . The company controlling the New Idanha recognized his ability and for five years he has remained in his present managerial capacity."

Running a hotel was not Grout's only business. He had farm property near Ontario, Oregon, and an investment in the King Hill irrigation project. Even with all those brain benders on his mind he often took time for fishing and hunting. His favorite fishing spots were Silver Creek and streams on Camas Prairie between Mountain Home and Fairfield.

His involvement at King Hill was told in the *Capital News:*

" 'There will be about 500 settlers plowing and setting out orchards on the King Hill tract as soon as spring opens,' declared C. H. Grout, manager of the Idanha hotel this morning on his return from a trip through the Medbury, Clover Creek and King Hill tract which he intends to improve this year. He is enthusiastic over the prospects of the new fruit region.

" 'That country is being transformed from a desert into a rich farming community,' continued Mr. Grout. 'You would be surprised at the amount of land that has been cleared and the plans being made for improvements. I saw canals and ditches ready for water to be turned into. . . . King Hill people are doing everything in their power to assist the settlers in the work of clearing the land and planting it to orchard. Having seen this country when it was covered with nothing but sagebrush, it certainly looked good to me to see the cleared land and the amount already under the plow.

" 'The same activity is true on the Clover Creek tract which promises to be one of the best in the southern part of the state. The new townsite of Teskeske is to be opened on this tract and all preparations have been made to make it one of the leading towns in that section of the country. Down in the Medbury tract there is a great deal of activity which means the planting of a great deal of the land to fruit. The new town of Hammett is also coming to the front and gives promise of being one of the very best.' "

Grout harvested legal problems as well as crops from his property. A farmhand named Schmidt filed suit in justice court for $150 he said Grout owed him. Grout said Schmidt wasn't working for him but for Joe Qualles, to whom Grout had leased a ranch near Bliss. According to Grout, the man who leased the ranch needed a hired man or two. Grout told Schmidt to apply. He got the job and was paid for one month out of the four he worked. One out of four didn't seem right, so he went to court. The outcome was a compromise; Grout and the tenant split the labor bill.

A much bigger issue hit the courts a little later. The state land board asked that a federal receiver be appointed to straighten out the tangled affairs of the King Hill Irrigation Company. Dreams of bountiful crops and healthy bank accounts had dissolved. By 1911 the glowing forecast by Grout proved too enthusiastic.

A newspaper article said the case was the result of a fight between the irrigation companies from the state under the Carey Act. Bondholders — mostly in the East — said irrigation ditches had been completed. The settlers said they didn't have water. Lawyers fired volleys of accusations, countercharges, stipulations, and bills of particulars, until Idaho and Philadelphia legal officers were knee-deep in folders, and courts were jammed with the residue. Just how Grout and others came out is hard to tell without an extensive search of court journals. However, it is reasonably safe to say that the King Hill project did not meet its touted potential. Furthermore, it appears that Grout got out of the farm business. He took his losses and devoted almost all his time to the Idanha.

But not quite all. Grout loved to fish. When he was not whipping up a new delight for the restaurant, he was likely to be catching trout. He told a reporter he was too nervous to put on bait so he relied on the fly. One of his trips was detailed by the *Capital News*. Grout and John McMillan, an owner of the Idanha, left at five o'clock in the morning in the McMillan car driven by a chauffeur. They reached Little Camas River, seventy-five miles away, in about five hours. Fishing was great. Grout said, "The way in which trout rose after the spawn bait used to attract them made it as easy to catch them as anything I know of."

"I confess that when it comes to fishing for trout with a fly the sport strikes me," said Grout. "It was simply a matter of hauling the fish in. But it was good sport. Of course we kept under the twenty-pound limit."

Bird hunting was another of his hobbies. He shot his share of sage grouse, turtle doves, and foolhens. When he varied the bag with turkey, he blasted his way into a mess of trouble. It was a practical joke that got out of hand.

Several days before Thanksgiving he went down the

valley to lay in a supply of quail. When he got back, his hunting jacket bulged. Telling noboby how many he had, hinting that he might have gone over the limit, he unloaded in his office. When the coast was clear he slipped down to the kitchen with an eighteen-pound turkey. He told the cook to dress it and roast it for Thanksgiving. All on the quiet, of course. Then, because he couldn't keep his secret, Grout leaked the tale to a friend. He said he was going through a cornfield when this enormous bird practically knocked him down. He shot in self-defense. The bird belonged to a farmer. Grout said he was sorry about the mistake, but he could not find the farmer to confess. So he decided to keep the bird and enjoy it.

Hunting stories being what they are, it was only a short time before an officer appeared at Grout's door. He had already been to the kitchen, seen the turkey, and heard from the farmer. Mr. Grout would have to go along to the police station. He did, with little protest. He was ordered to court. Heavy bail was specified. Because he didn't have the cash and the police sergeant would not take a check, Grout was locked in a cell. He sat there repenting of his sins. In a few minutes he heard the voices of old friends. One by one his pals dropped by, expressing shock at the disgraceful conduct of their friend. Finally, Grout got in touch with his butcher, who explained to the police that it was all a joke. Grout had bought the turkey.

Out of jail, but more than a little out of sorts with his fellows because his stunt had gone too far, he relented enough to treat the gang to drinks and cigars. In retaliation he said he would eat the Thanksgiving turkey alone.

Because of his jovial manner, combined with a strong baritone, Grout was a natural for the Elks Minstrels. He cavorted as a black-face end man in several productions. Touted in high-octane ads as "Pop" Grout, America's leading matinee idol from Inkom, he cracked jokes and sang ditties. The program was first put on at Pocatello, where Grout had spent a lot of time in the dining car business.

On the Idanha front, things of importance were taking

place. The big switch was in the dining room. Grout fired all the Negro waiters and replaced them with white girls. Racial questions were common in those days. When the Idanha opened, it refused to employ Chinese. Hardly any other public place did, either. Some cafes and hotels that had Chinese help were boycotted. As the need for cheap workers continued, there was a trend to Negro men and women instead of Orientals. Then, as was shown in the Idanha about 1910, white workers made such a fuss they took many jobs from blacks.

Grout said the change was made at the solicitation of the traveling public. "The hungry traveler who steps into the attractive cafe now," he said, "will be served by deft-handed maids in pretty uniforms of black and white."

Rooms upstairs were renovated. New furniture was placed in the parlor. Much of the furniture was replaced with antique oak upholstered in leather. The big upper verandah opening from the parlor was furnished with porch furniture, making "an ideal resting place either morning or evening."

The Idanha also announced plans to build an annex on Tenth and Idaho, a block north, to provide rooms on three or four stories. It would be connected to the main hotel by a closed walkway over the alley. Grout said the development would advance the intention of the Idanha to maintain its place as the leading hotel in Idaho. The statement had reference to the opening of the Owyhee in 1910. The Idanha was faced, too, with the prospect of additional competition from the Boise Hotel Company, which had started plans in 1907 and was offering hints in 1910 that it would soon have its "big tourist hostelry" in the vacant property between Eighth and Ninth streets between Jefferson and State.

The annex to the Idanha was not built. The hotel sold the corner. On the Boise Hotel front, progress was slow, the hotel was finally constructed but twenty years later.

Grout was famous for Idanha food. He took pains to load his tables with the best. The menu for the 1910 Christmas dinner, at the peak of his career, shows the style he offered.

Idaho Historical Society

Hotel Boise was completed in 1930, more than 20 years after it was on the drawing board. Today it is the Hoff Building with shops and cafes. It is no longer a hotel.

A copy is included among the illustrations. Here's the lineup:

Canapes de jambon au diable, Olympic oyster cocktail, rice tomato soup, consomme, chiffonade, ripe olives, celery, dill pickles, salmon, trout, shrimp sauce, potato en glace, small patties volunteer style, stuffed tame duck a la Britannica, chocolate eclairs, cream sauce, succotash, green peas, Roman punch, roast prime ribs of beef au jus, roast suckling pig a l'anglaise, roast young turkey, cranberry sauce, mashed potato, spinach with egg, crab salad en mayonnaise, steamed fruit pudding, brandy sauce, hot mince pie, lemon meringue pie, tutti-frutti ice cream, assorted cakes, Swiss cheese, Roquefort cheese, Bent's crackers, sweet cider, coffee, tea, milk.

The menu reflects the impression made on Grout by the meal served to William Howard Taft when the host of the Idanha was a freshman in the business. The menu was reprinted many years later on a Christmas card issued by the Broadbent Estate when it owned the Idanha.

Oh, yes, how about the cost of that Christmas dinner at the Idanha? Would you believe one dollar? That's what it was. Of course the price went up if you took a split of red or white wine. That brought it to $1.25.

Grout was keen on new things. He welcomed mechanical advances which knocked out the enunciator that had been such a hit at the Idanha. He rejoiced in and spent bundles of money on new plumbing. He was among the first airplane believers in Idaho. At a time when planes were laughed at, he praised them, predicting they would

Main Street about 1910. The turreted Idanha is at the left.

Idaho Historical Society

catch up with or replace the auto, as the auto had done away with the horse.

Believers and scoffers had a chance to see what aviation could do, at an airplane-auto extravaganza in Boise in April 1911. Walter Brookings brought a Wright biplane to race Frank Irving's Buick at the Intermountain Fairgrounds for a $1,000 prize. The mile race was to be the main attraction of a show to introduce planes.

As a means of promoting the show, managers announced that a local citizen of prominence would be a passenger on the first flight over the city. A guessing game narrowed the nominees to the governor, the attorney general, the mayor, and the secretary of state. None won. Brookings warmed up his motor, stepped into the waiting crowd, and tapped Charles Grout. The popular host of Boise's favorite hotel was delighted. He put on the coveralls, leather jacket, and helmet. He waved to the crowd and climbed aboard. A cheer went up.

The plane didn't. Brookings gave it the gun. It rose a few feet and settled to earth like a wounded goose. The aviator tried it again. Same result. No takeoff. Brookings taxied back to the crowd and turned off the engine.

"Sorry," he said, "I guess you're too heavy."

Grout dismounted. A lighter resident took his place for a short hop over the fairgrounds. Recovering quickly from his disappointment, Grout is reported to have said he was sorry he was too big but that his glorious pounds were a product of meals at the Idanha.

In any event, weather was windy and cold. Fat man or no fat man, it was a poor time to fly. Next day Brookings made what was described as a magnificent flight. He was in the air 13 minutes at more than 300 feet. The event was proclaimed the first flight in Idaho. The little bounce along the fairgrounds the previous day did not qualify as a real airborne journey.

Except for the flight, the show was a fizzle. The race between plane and car was cancelled. Aviators left early for another date. A small crowd hung around to see W. H.

THE Idan-ha
BOISE, IDAHO.
IDAN-HA HOTEL CO. LTD. PROPS.
CHARLES H GROUT MGR

Special Dinner $1.00

WITH SPLIT OF RED OR WHITE WINE $1.25
SERVED FROM 5:30 TO 8:00

MONDAY, DECEMBER 26, 1910

Canapes, de Jambon, a la Diable

Olympia Oyster Cocktail

Rice Tomato — *Consomme, Chiffonade*
Ripe Olives — *Celery* — *Dill Pickles*

Salmon Trout, Shrimp Sauce
Potato, en Glace

Small Patties, Voluteer Style
Stuffed Tame Duck, a la Britannica
Chocolate Eclairs, Cream Sauce

Succotash — *Green Peas*

Roman Punch

Roast Prime Ribs of Beef, au Jus
Roast Suckling Pig, a l'Anglaise
Roast Young Turkey, Cranberry Sauce

Potato, Mashed — *Spinach with Egg*

Crab Salad, en Mayonnaise

Steamed Fruit Pudding, Brandy Sauce
Hot Mince Pie — *Lemon Meringue Pie*
Tutti Frutti Ice Cream and Assorted Cakes

Swiss Cheese — *Roquefort Cheese*

Bent's Crackers

Sweet Cider — *Coffee* — *Tea* — *Milk*

TIMES HAVE CHANGED,

BUT . . .

OUR MESSAGE REMAINS THE SAME!

Merry Christmas

and

Happy New Year

from

All of Us at Broadbent

A Merry Christmas.

Christmas menu, 1910

Estabrook of Idaho City race his big steamer against Irving's Buick. Estabrook took a fourteen-second handicap because his car was almost twice as powerful as the Buick. He won easily. A disgusted reporter said it was more like a parade than a race. He called the whole thing a bore.

In 1912 Grout had throat trouble. He was granted leave to be treated at the Mayo Clinic. Doctors cleared up the difficulty. He returned in a few weeks to his usual duties. During his absence some of his work was done by J. V. Sweetman, chief clerk. Mr. and Mrs. Grout had served the wedding breakfast when Sweetman married Myrtle Newell. Sweetman had been president of the Greeters of Idaho. In a later era he was manager of the Idanha.

Grout was manager until the end of December 1913. He spent a few months at Seaside, Oregon, on vacation and helping out at a beach resort. He then returned to Idaho as manager of the Guyer Hot Springs Hotel at Hailey, probably eager to return to the area near Silver Creek where he had enjoyed fishing and where he continued to toss a fly. In his Wood River period Grout added to his fame by putting on a feast at the Hot Springs for James McDonald that would have done credit to Roman rulers. In addition to the food — the finest that domestic and foreign markets afforded — there was entertainment rated by a society editor as "something from the *Midsummer Night's Dream.*"

Always bubbling with ideas to advance hotel and restaurant business, Grout whipped up a plan to link several hotels in a scenic area in a series of special events at bargain prices. For instance, a single guest or a group would spend a couple of days at the Hiawatha in Hailey, go on to Ketchum for a hot bath and the night, on to Redfish Lake where fishing would be an attraction added to room and board, on to Stanley for the same treats, on to Robinson Bar for swimming, fishing, and hunting in season, and then to Salmon City or Challis. Transportation would be provided by automobiles leased to the travel company. One or two of the hotels Grout approached liked the idea. Others were cool. What was probably the first package deal in the travel business in Idaho failed to take hold. It was not until Grout had gone to his reward that tourism became a tremendous boon to hotels. He was ahead of his time. For one thing, roads were terrible. For another, people liked to drive their own cars loaded with tents, pots, pans, and spare tires.

The IDAN-HA

The big event on the hotel front in 1910 was the opening of the Owyhee on May 9. It was a challenge to the McMillans of the Idanha, who had ruled the roost without serious competition for nearly a decade. Manager Grout had reason to be anxious, too. If the new hotel proved to be the pleasure palace it was cracked up to be, Grout might lose his position as the number one host. His chief rival was E. W. Schubert, remembered by the Idanha as one of its former managers and by the community as a genial greeter at both the Idanha and the old Overland.

The Owyhee pulled out all the stops for a grand entrance into the world of bed and board. Gov. James Brady was among the distinguished guests at the ribbon cutting. Throngs streamed through the modern building at Eleventh and Main, just a block from the Idanha. Visitors were given details about the two hundred bedrooms, three dining rooms, a magnificent lobby with pillars like those in the statehouse, and retiring rooms for ladies and gentlemen. At an appointed hour, keys of the hotel were presented to Governor Brady by seven-year-old Zella Dawson. The governor dropped them into a furnace. Manager Schubert said they were forever burned. The Boise High

School band played. A master of ceremonies told the crowd that "Owyhee" meant "friendly greeting," signifying the fellowship of pioneers. Perhaps so. Common belief, based on reliable research, is that "Owyhee" is a derivation of "Hawaii" because some natives of the islands worked in southern Idaho, giving the name to Owyhee County and thence to the hotel. Proprietors of the Idanha were in no position to poke fun at the "friendly greeting" translation. The name of their own place did not stand up under inspection. So it was a case of a new "aloha" to old "healing waters."

J. E. Tourtelotte was the architect of the Owyhee. Jack Cody was construction superintendent. Cody Field on Warm Springs Avenue, where East Junior High now stands, was for many years a baseball and football ground.

Opening of the Owyhee had one hitch. Manager Schubert proudly announced that the kitchen had the finest equipment and culinary department this side of Chicago. He urged people to try the fare. He would have been glad to eat his words. No meals could be served for two days because the china had not arrived. Well, it had arrived, but somebody had forgotten to unpack it!

The several dining rooms were attractive, tastefully furnished, and as stylish as anything in Boise, putting Grout on his toes to keep pace. Undaunted, the Idanha advertised itself on the day of the Owyhee opening as "Idaho's leading hotel. Rooms $1 to $3." To maintain his reputation in the dining field against the finger bowls and fine linen of the Owyhee, Grout created new delights, including such baronial gorges as his Christmas dinner the first winter after the Owyhee opened.

A couple of months later, the Owyhee added a roof garden. The patio-style quarters, overlooking the city, served afternoon tea in British fashion and more hearty meals — mostly to special parties. It became *the* place for Society with a capital S. The Rose Room downstairs off the stately lobby was noted for its napery, fresh flowers, and the charming efficiency, in more recent times, of such waiters as the late Andy Horton. But the Roof Garden had the spell of cosmopolitan luxury. The well-heeled, accompanied by the nonheeled who enjoyed being in important company, patronized the roof.

While liquor was legal, cocktails were served. When Idaho went dry, cocktails were still sold. The Roof Garden was raided. By the time the legal entanglement was unraveled, the appeal of the garden had faded. Repeal of the Eighteenth Amendment came too late. Other drinkeries and snuggeries had siphoned off the customers.

In the beginning, Schubert was president of the Owyhee Hotel Company. Harry Falk was secretary and Leo J. Falk treasurer. Within a short time the Falks became owners in fact, rather than financial backers of Schubert.

The Owyhee continued as one of Boise's leading hotels until the 1970s, when it was taken over by a food-processing company. Computers were installed in the basement, eliminating, among other things, the Dungeon Room, where many a robust occasion was enjoyed by diners beguiled by leering figurines perched on shelves around the hall.

Bits and pieces of the old Owyhee still remain. There is a motel that makes use of part of the hotel, plus annexes, and dining rooms handy to bars. The grand old lobby is divided into offices. The Arid Club, Boise's most exclusive men's social enterprise, has moved to another building.

Some of the lobby is still there. It is only a fraction of the impressive space that seated more than a thousand persons on its floor and in the balcony. What is left brings back memories of Lincoln Day banquets at which national leaders said good things about the GOP and Ralph Breshears read the Gettysburg Address so stirringly that lumps rose even in Democratic throats. The lobby was also the scene of Knife and Fork Club addresses by such renowned men as Carl Sandburg, Will Durant, and Billy Mitchell, the fiery air force general.

The Idanha did not have space for such affairs. However, the Idanha is still there; the old Owyhee isn't. The Idanha, which shared in the "friendly greeting" in 1910, bade it a "friendly goodbye."

The IDAN-HA

Getting back to the history of the Idanha, many things other than the arrival of the Owyhee were taking place in and around the McMillan inn. The Idanha had a fire scare in 1910 when the nearby Wheeler-Motter Building burned. The hotel was not damaged.

John McMillan arranged a celebration for Senator Borah to honor him for his support of a bill providing $20 million for western reclamation. He planned a parade from the railway station to the Idanha, where Borah would speak from the same verandah where he appeared after his vindication in the land fraud action. Everybody thought the idea was great except Borah. He vetoed the deal, exercising his tendency to dissent, which members of his party and the opposition came to regard as par. In spite of his decline, a crowd met him. He refused to ride in an auto like a conquering hero. He walked to the hotel, chatted with friends, then slipped out to his office.

Angry women marched on the hotel in 1911. They had no quarrel with the Idanha but were boiling because a visitor named George Kingswell had said some nasty things about woman's suffrage. He opposed equal rights for women. He said the country "wants women more lovable instead of being poor imitations of men." He escaped back to his Texas home without mayhem.

Ruben C. Moore, coast artillery, and Miss C. A. Moore, his sister, were reunited at the Idanha after a separation of more than twenty years. They hadn't had much chance to get together because he was on duty in various posts and she was a traveling salesman — in fact, she was said to be the oldest traveling salesman in the country. Saleslady? Not her. She worked a man's world and accepted their terms.

There was embarrassment when a Negro janitor who worked for the telephone company and did an occasional job for the Idanha shot at a lady friend three times because she would not do his laundry or accept his attentions. One shot hit her in the neck, another in the arm, and the third missed. The unwashed and unloved suitor then shot himself above the heart. He recovered and so did she.

The morning of September 14, 1909, brought a shocking surprise to the Idanha. A Peasley Transfer Company team ran away on Tenth Street. Horses and wagon crashed into the heavy posts supporting the balcony. It crashed to the street. Several pedestrians narrowly escaped. A reconstruction of the accident by witnesses said one wheel struck a post, breaking it off. The second post gave way. Neither of the horses was injured. Debris of the balcony blocked the entrance several hours. The balcony was restored. Some years later it was taken down. Mrs. Ansgar Johnson, manager, said it was serving no purpose. The balcony was no longer needed for speeches, and pedestrians kept bumping into it.

The balcony was smashed by the transfer wagon just a day before the Idanha played an important part in one of Boise's most impressive Chinese weddings. Fon Tui Bow, a Boise merchant of prominence, married Chin Chee of Port Townsend, Washington. More than five hundred were invited to the wedding at the Chinese Temple on Idaho Street. The bride stayed at the Idanha with her maid, who doubled as interpreter and had the appropriate name of Ah

Sai. In an interview with *The Statesman* the bride spoke thus, as passed on by the interpreter:

"She say she marry big man who got some money and only one wife. When man has more than one wife women talk too much and get jealousies. One wife nobody make trouble. Keep her mouth shut and have good time."

Acceptance of the charming Chinese bride was evidence of a change in hotel policy. At the beginning, Chinese were not allowed to take rooms. They were not even permitted to perform menial jobs.

A few years later the Idanha was unhappy because one of its customers was arrested on a charge of embezzlement. The incident has gone down in oral history as the case of the Mounted Police Muff. F. S. Washburn, Portland, registered at the hotel on a winter day. He was soon taken into custody by Boise officers acting on tips from the Northwest Mounted Police that he was wanted for embezzling $1,000 in Vancover. A private sleuth hired by the Mounties had traced him to Boise. The detective mingled with guests at the Idanha and convinced himself that Washburn was his man. A Canadian officer hastened to Boise to work out extradition.

Washburn demurred. He insisted he had nothing to do with the missing money in Vancouver. He said he was a salesman for an auto-lock company. He had never been in Canada.

Mounted police and Idaho officers were skeptical. What proof did Washburn have? A light dawned. When, he asked, did this embezzlement take place? A date was given. "Good," said Washburn, "I can prove I was not there." He phoned William Sweet of the Sweet-Teller Hardware Company in Boise.

"Remember a baseball game your team played in Walla Walla last July?" he asked. "I'm Washburn. Remember?"

"Sure do," replied Sweet. "You're the umpire that gave us a bad time."

"Sorry about that, but you can get me out of a hole now. Tell this policeman where I was."

Sweet confirmed the alibi. Case closed. The mounted police always gets its man. Sometimes the wrong man.

Four alumni from the University of Virginia had a chance to catch up on their eating at the Idanha Cafe in the summer of 1910. They were traveling around the world by foot, boat, car, rickshaw, or whatever. They said that on an African desert they had been without food for seven days when their camels got away. They survived on dried beans. Manager Grout saw to it they had more sustaining food at his table.

Mr. and Mrs. Adolph Topperwein of San Antonio, billed as the best marksmen in the world, gave an exhibition of rifle and shotgun magic at Boise Barracks in the summer of 1910. They amazed 1,500 spectators by carving profiles of Indians with .22 shots and breaking dozens of tossed eggs with shotgun blasts without leaving a single yolk for an omelette. After the show they displayed their guns at the Idanha and enjoyed a snack with Grout, also no slouch with a shotgun.

The Idanha took part, indirectly, in a civic function that same year. Robert Aikman, a director, helped dedicate a drinking fountain presented to the city by the W.C.T.U. Aikman was a member of the city council. The fountain honors Mrs. Mary Tolles, an antisaloon worker who died in Boise in 1909. When the old city hall was knocked down, the fountain was moved to the new building.

One of Boise's most important musical events of the period was a concert by the New York Symphony Orchestra under the direction of Walter Damrosch. Boise's leading hotel was filled with the sounds of violinists, horn players, and drummers keeping their instruments in shape for the performance. The lobby bulged with luggage. Conversation in the cafe was so full of Brahms, Mozart, and Bach that waiters could hardly hear orders for soup and salad. The program was a smashing success, helping to launch Boise's appreciation of great music and to pave the way for the philharmonic orchestra that gives the city a place of distinction today.

There was speculation at the time and since as to why Madame Nordica, the opera singer, passed up a chance to hear the New York Symphony in Boise, choosing instead to see a circus. The circumstance makes her visit more mysterious than ever.

Scholarship was very much in the picture at the Idanha, along with classical music and fancy marksmanship. Among the numerous occasions on which the hotel did its bit for education was the convention of county superintendents at Thanksgiving in 1910. Many superintendents stayed at the Idanha. A lucky few in the upper echelons were guests of the manager at a turkey dinner. The convention was notable for a resolution asking that dances be prohibited in public schools. Educators took the issue to the legislature, where it was batted about for several sessions. The matter was finally left to the judgment of school boards. Dancing is still a subject of debate.

A more interesting event for many old-timers that holiday was the visit by A. H. Boomer, former agent for the Northwest Stage Line. He greeted friends at the hotel and elsewhere about town, expressing regret that his current home in New York was so far from his old stomping grounds.

Fairly fresh memories of the Harry Orchard excitement were brought into sharper focus at that time by the death in California of Harry Crane, a reporter who had covered the trial for *The Statesman*. Crane was killed in the bombing of the *Los Angeles Times*.

A meal at the Idanha was a treat for men, women, and children. Lawrence Hannifin, long-time operator (with his brother John) of Hannifin's Cigar Store, remembers a birthday dinner he almost got when he was a small boy. Hannifin, now retired, was recently asked what he knew about early times at the hotel. At first he said he knew nothing whatever. Then he warmed up. Nostalgia bloomed. What he remembered most about a certain day when he was very small, he said, were the horses. The horses? Well, they weren't exactly at the hotel, but they were part of his gift at the Idanha.

"I had a new suit," he said. "It was a very special occasion. And my dad gave me sixty-five cents. Because I was feeling so good and wanted to work up more appetite I went to one of my favorite places before dinner — the livery stable. It was a couple of blocks from the hotel, about where the Shrine Club is today. They had lots of horses, mostly big ones that hauled loads around town. I knew most of them by name. So I went down there to show them my new suit. I walked up and down the stall talking to one horse after another and petting them. They were wonderful horses.

"I must have gone down all the walkways two or three times. I helped the stable hands move a load or two of manure, too. It was a very big day. Pretty soon I guessed I had better go to dinner. I walked into the dining room and sat down. Quite a few people were there. They started sniffing and looking at me. I thought maybe they thought I didn't have sixty-five cents. I showed them the money. They still sniffed and waved their napkins in the air like they were too hot. Then somebody said 'Little boy, you don't smell very good.' I probably didn't, but I didn't care much. Those big horses meant more to me than a dinner. And I still had the sixty-five cents."

Jerry Hannifin, son of John and now a correspondent for *Time* magazine in Washington, D.C., made use of the Idanha for a different purpose. He says when he was in grade school, or perhaps a little later, the gang used to have fistfights down by the railway tracks. No particular reason, just fights like boys always have for the heck of it. When they had enough of clobbering each other they went to the Idanha basement to mop up the blood and wash their grubby faces. There was then, and still is, a tiled washroom. "It was almost worth the black eyes and split lips to go down there and clean up," Hannifin says. The gang thought of it as the Idanha first-aid station.

The fancy facilities were a source of irritation to Mrs.

Ansgar Johnson while she managed the hotel in later years. Pay toilets were installed. The Idanha had a contract with the pay-toilet firm, which split the take with the hotel. After keeping careful accounts and paying the firm its share for several years, Mrs. Johnson asked her lawyer to see about a better arrangement. He studied the documents. "Roxie," the attorney said, "that contract expired five years ago." Mrs. Johnson was not amused.

Gov. Moses Alexander proclaimed a holiday on Armistice Day 1918. More than ten thousand people shouted, marched, blew whistles, and popped firecrackers. A parade through the business district was supposed to be the main event. It was more of a mob scene. A band led the way. Followers wandered all over the place in jubilant disorder. Kaiser Bill was burned in effigy in front of the Idanha. The corner of Tenth and Main was the center of the tumult. Banners carried such slogans as "The Kaiser has the flu. He has flown," and "We got the Kaiser's goat." The latter was displayed above a goat that did not like anything about the festivities.

The line of march — if a meandering rabble can be called a line — included scores of hastily decorated autos. Bunting flew on the Idanha porch and from upper stories of other hotels and businesses. Confetti was ankle deep. Gov. Elect D. W. Davis delivered a short talk. So did Governor Alexander. They didn't speak long because nobody was in a listening mood. The wife of a Boise barber fell out of a car while celebrating. She was killed.

A good many citizens were caught without confetti or firecrackers because they didn't think the war would be over in November. They made up for it with what seemed like tons of talcum powder. A news account said the street smelled ladylike.

At the time of the armistice the Idanha advertised that it was "The leading Hotel of Boise. In Center of Everything Commercial and Stockgrowers Headquarters. One Dollar and Up. Join a Thrift Stamp Club." The reference to thrift

Mrs. Ansgar Johnson (Roxie McMillan) managed the hotel through critical years in the innkeeping business.

stamps was evidence that the hotel had done its bit for liberty bonds and other programs to help finance the war.

John McMillan found a verse in the hotel lobby about a month later that told how at least one man felt about conditions in the labor market. The poem, written on hotel stationery and tossed into the wastebasket, said:

> Farm work is hard work sure
> Tired bones and muscles are hard to endure.
> At night you seek your weary couch
> At 5 A.M. you awake with a grouch.
> You work all day 'till 9 or half past
> And wonder how long you'll last.
> It may do for youth but for one past 63
> It's wearying and may soon set a busy soul free.
> I find ranch work continuous drudgery
> And the pay of a country gentleman humbuggery.

The thought brought many chuckles. However, the quality was not up to the poems of Eugene Field, read at the Idanha on an earlier occasion by his brother. It was one stop on a tour to encourage the arts in general, also to call specific attention to the noted poet, who made his start in Denver. In the cultural line it is worth noting that Pablo Casals, who became the world's greatest cellist, was in Boise for a concert in 1919. He was then believed to be a "potential artist." He played in Boise about forty years later. Where he stayed is not known. Idanha partisans liked to believe he practiced his cello in their inn. If he did he joins a roster or renowned musicians, orators, actors, entertainers, and statesmen who have registered.

One guest, by no means in that category and a patron the Idanha would like to forget, was among the customers soon after World War I. He was given a room by a good Samaritan who took compassion on his plight. It seems Mr. Doe — who gave a phony name at the hotel — convinced a man he met on the train that he had lost his wallet, suitcase, and everything to some scamp who unloaded his goods at a stop down the line. He put up such an appealing case the businessman let him share his room. He also took the unfortunate traveler to dinner. Early in the morning, while it was still dark, the befriended gent slipped out. He took with him $530 belonging to his roommate. He hired a taxi to take him to Ontario. Arrested there on the basis of information from the hotel in Boise and the taxi driver, he was hauled back to Idaho. He pungled up $270 to the man he robbed. He suffered a jail sentence, but that did not compensate the Samaritan.

John McMillan ran for mayor in 1919. He had been a member of the legislature, postmaster, and city councilman. One of his ads said he favored aggressive, positive, and progressive programs. He favored purchase of Elm Grove Park, the leasing of Columbia Park, and improvement of Julia Davis Park. He wanted a good road to Arrowrock. He urged completion of the statehouse. He said the city council should reopen the ladies' rest room at the city hall.

At the election in April he led the field, but there were so many candidates with a few votes he did not get a majority. McMillan had 1,368 votes to 1,291 for Ern Eagleson. In the runoff, Eagleson won by a margin of about 600. The ladies' rest room was opened anyhow.

The IDAN-HA

An important chapter in the history of the Idanha began in 1920. George Cordes took a ten-year lease on the cafeteria and cafe. After Grout concluded his term as manager in 1913 the dining rooms were operated by the McMillans and J. V. Sweetman, except for brief period when they were leased to H. J. Thompson.

Cordes was a natural for the restaurant business. He was born in Greece. In his youth he was an athlete. He almost made the Greek Olympic team as a Marathon runner, running on the original course.

Eager to come to America, he worked his way on a freighter. To his dismay he discovered jobs in the East were scarce. Even in Greek restaurants he had only an occasional chore, usually at washing dishes or swamping out. So Cordes drifted to the West. He worked on section gangs. He tried house-to-house selling. He took a whack at mining. Nothing clicked.

On a bleak winter day in Wyoming town he hit bottom. He was broke, out of work, at the end of his string. Like a forlorn, freezing character in an O'Henry story he devoured a meal in a cafe and told the boss he couldn't pay. The proprietor said it was okay; he figured Cordes was on the bum.

With a hot meal under his belt and his spirits lifted by human kindness, Cordes resolved to make something of himself and to pay back to others what had been given to him. If he was ever in a position to feed the hungry, he vowed, he would do his best to help them. How thoroughly he succeeded is well understood by all who knew him for many years at Boise restaurants, mainly the Idanha.

Cordes found work, saved a bit of money, and came to Boise to get into a business more suited to his nationality and talents than working on a section gang. In 1912 he opened the Up-to-Date, a fruit stand at 1010 Main. He sold candy, cigars, and magazines, as well as apples and oranges. The stand prospered. He served sandwiches and other light lunches. He expanded the shop to take care of customers in back rooms as well as up front. The Up-to-Date was very close to the Rose Bud, a confectionery store run by Otto Johnson and Robert Freeman. The two places drew traffic profitable to both. The Rose Bud served the most delicious ice cream in the world. The specialty had the flavor of crushed rose petals blended with ambrosia. Boys fortunate enough to have lived in that time recall the triple delight of memorable occasions when a quarter was a fortune. One dime for streetcar fare, with a transfer home if it was engineered properly. Another dime for a swim at the Nat. One nickle for a cone at the Rose Bud. That was an afternoon on Mount Olympus.

Although business at the Up-to-Date was gratifying, Cordes wanted to go into the restaurant trade in a larger way. In 1920 he took over the cafeteria and cafe at the Idanha. The cafeteria occupied the north end of the first floor, approximately the area of Peter Schott's Restaurant in 1983. The cafe was to the immediate east of the lobby. For many years it was connected to the lobby by a hall and a few stairsteps. The cafeteria is now often confused with an ingenious mechanical restaurant. It should not be. The facility at the Idanha was a cafeteria where customers did the walking and the food stood still. The genuine Mechanafe was on Eighth Street near Bannock. The proprietor was Mrs. Gertrude McDevitt, one-time director of the Idaho Historical Museum. The Mechanafe prospered for a time in the 1930s, charging something like sixty cents for all you could eat. Portions of everything from soup to pie kept coming by on an endless-belt conveyor. Diners could slip empty plates back onto the conveyor and clear their consciences of gluttony. Athletic teams were partly responsible for the demise of the eatery. Football squads from outlaying towns descended on the place, devouring everything that moved. Very little was left for other diners.

Cordes did not have that problem with his cafeteria. Customers made one trip, paid the tab, and found a seat. That was it.

The cafe was fancier. A horseshoe counter and tables seated a good many patrons. Waitresses were kept busy. Cordes could not maintain the culinary pace set by Grout, the trencherman, on his festival occasions. In general his meals were more on the meat-and-potatoes side than the epicurean mysteries of his noted predecessor. He did serve adequate portions of wholesome food.

His most vigorous competitor was Kelly's Club Cafe, 823 Main, a popular restaurant operated by Jim Kelly, who had started his career peddling goodies from a push cart. Brand's Cafe in a basement room at Ninth and Main was gone by that time. A. W. Brand had served a discriminating clientelle for a good many years, catering to the after-the-theatre crowd. Brand got attention with his ads. Some of them read: "You like my meals if you don't like me. You do read my ads. Keep coming to Brand's."

One Idanha Thanksgiving menu, à la Cordes, started with the traditional oyster cocktail, followed by mock turtle soup and filet of sole and working through suckling pig, roast turkey, and vegetables to Idanha special salade (with the "e"), three kinds of pie, Camembert, and demitasse. Among those eating that repast was David Starr Jordan, a famous educator, in Boise for a state teachers' convention. Sharing the platform, and possibly the Idanha table, was Alfred Upham, president of the University of Idaho.

All respectable cafes in Boise were keen on oysters. If they didn't have two or three kinds they kept still. Blue Points and Olympics were top choices, frequently served on the half shell.

Here's a sample of Kelly's later fare — the menu for Thanksgiving, 1925: Ada County turkey, noisette of roast pork tenderloin with sauce sultana; prime rib of beef, boiled capon, baked sugar-cured ham southern, roast goose with apple compote, Waldorf salad, mashed potatoes, Hubbard squash, Thanksgiving pudding, numerous pies, ice cream coffee. Music was by Miss DeVine and orchestra. For a buck and a quarter it wasn't steep. Oysters and caviar were out of range.

Cordes was noted for two things: athletic teams and free dinners at Christmas, New Year's, and Thanksgiving.

Take the sports first.

Cordes was manager of a baseball team in the Alfalfa League that won championships. His outfit playing under the banner of the Up-to-Date around 1916 to 1919 was classy enough to take on and beat the semipros in Boise Valley. Mountain Home, Emmett, and other clubs that had been doing their stuff in Walter ("Spider") Johnson's time, regrouped to give battle. The Up-to-Dates prevailed often enough to boast they were cock of the walk.

Cordes then turned to basketball. He recruited stars from college and high school ranks to build a club that was the equal of anything in the state. Well, almost. But it was a rare night that the Up-to-Dates took a trimming. They had close calls against the Comets of Rupert, which featured several great players. They lost a disputed game to the Payette Legion by one point. Cordes was scorekeeper as well as manager. After the final bucket beat him he recounted and proclaimed that his boys had prevailed by a basket he had failed to record. His protest was overruled. In spite of a loss now and then, the Up-to-Dates won two championships in a row.

In the spring of 1919 they challenged the University of Idaho, with W. C. Bleamaster as coach. The Vandals accepted. The game was played in Boise High School gym. The place pleased Cordes; he chose it. There wasn't much choice. The other available floor was at the YMCA, where the court was even cozier than the sardine can at the high school. The high school gym had a ceiling about ten feet high and walls so close to the boundary lines that players could hardly move without losing a patch of skin. The Up-to-Dates were used to it; it was their home cave. They knew how to bank shots off the grills protecting ceiling lights. They were handy at bouncing passes off the walls when the referee couldn't see what was happening.

The Vandals said the place was terrible, although they had been playing in the cracker box at the old university gym, which was only a little bigger than the one in Boise. That gym, where Idaho won several western titles, has been converted into a classroom. Memorial gym replaced it and since then has been succeeded by the Kibbie Dome.

About two hundred fans turned out for the battle in Boise. That was near capacity. At the start, the Vandals had a terrible time. They were crushed under the basket, bounced along the walls, and generally treated like public enemies. The starting lineup for Cordes — Reynolds, Bailey, Cobley, Smith, and Tolman — followed a game plan that called for as much mayhem as possible. The strategy worked reasonably well. It was not up to the usual punishing level because a man named Fletcher was out with the mumps. Bailey, who took his place, was not as familiar with the shoulder-skinning exercises as the others.

Idaho absorbed all the punishment it thought reasonable before replying in kind. The Vandal team of Moe, Hunter, Perrine, Marden, and Lindley got tough. Their muscle, superior court skill, and excellent condition wore down the locals. The final score was 68 to 28 for Idaho. Coach Bleamaster and Ernest Lindley, university president, spoke at a high school assembly next morning. Lindley expressed appreciation to the Vandal team, not failing to note that one of the stars was his son, who became a writer for a national news magazine. Bleamaster forgave the

Up-to-Dates for their rough tactics. He said he hoped the Vandals would be invited to Boise again.

They were. The Idaho team of 1922, one of the best in the school's history, came to Boise in March to test the All Stars. The Vandals had won two championships that winter. They were tops in the Pacific Coast and Northwestern conferences. Representing the West they went to the first national tournament at Indianapolis, where they lost to Kalamazoo, 38 to 32. Wabash College defeated Kalamazoo in the final game.

The high-voltage Vandals were a big drawing card, as well as formidable competition for the best Boise could muster. Cordes no longer had his Up-to-Dates; he was devoting most of his time to the dining rooms at the Idanha. He had a ten-year lease, but management did not always see eye-to-eye with Cordes. There was a feeling that too much attention to athletics might reduce patronage at the hotel. Cordes did find time to help a committee of sports fans collect a team of active players, recent college stars, has-beens, and young hopefuls.

The field of battle was moved from the tiny high school gym to the White City pavilion, part of the entertainment complex run by Gladden Hull. It was much better. It seated many more people. It was larger and had a ceiling that permitted shots farther than ten feet from the hoop. Nearly one thousand people turned out.

Jim Keane, a former Vandal player and Boise High School coach, was coach of the All Stars. David McMillan, the Vandal coach, had a squad of all-time greats. He trotted out Rich Fox, Al Fox, Oz Thompson, Bill Gartin, Percy Steiner, Harold Telford, Harry Edwards, Adrian Nelson, and Henry Canine. Bill Gartin, then of Caldwell and now of Boise, is the last survivor.

Moscow people take pride in the fact that the Fox brothers, Thompson, Steiner, Edwards, and Nelson were all Moscow boys who played on teams that won state championships for Moscow High School.

The All Stars were primarily former Vandals. Their high

scorer was Squinty Hunter. Ward Wyman, also a former Vandal, had an outstanding night. Coach Keane played a few minutes. Others doing their stuff were Curly Douglas and Ed McLeod. Al Fox of the Vandals was high with eighteen points, about half on free throws, which were then tossed by a designated foul shooter. Idaho won, 52 to 22.

Cordes got back into the act by giving a dinner for the local players and as many visitors as could spare the time. Among those honored was Homer Huddelson, the referee. He had handled some Up-to-Date games. For many years he was an official at high school tournaments and was known for his strict control. When he called a foul, he could be heard for blocks. He pointed a finger at the offender, fixing an angry eye on him as though he had violated all Ten Commandments and was a candidate for hellfire. Many a high school player confessed he was more in fear of Homer's wrath than losing a game.

The University of Idaho won the Pacific Coast Conference again in 1923. Cordes and company didn't cook up another Boise game. One reason was that most of the basketball fever was focused on the high school. Boise had been beaten twice by Oakley but was selected for the state tournament at Moscow in place of Driggs, a powerhouse whose players were down with the flu. Weston, a previous champ, could not compete because its schedule was in a shambles. In any event, Coeur d'Alene knocked out Boise by one point. Then Boise lost another in the double-elimination. Oakley beat Moscow. Next day Moscow beat Oakley. Oakley beat Coeur d'Alene. In its third game against Oakley that weekend, Moscow won the title.

All this basketball stuff may seem irrelevant to the Idanha. It was not. Cordes was a loyal supporter of the Boise team, suggesting diets and offering training tables. In spite of the fact that much of his advice was ignored, he kept an eye on prospects for another basketball team that he expected to launch. Sad to say, it didn't get off the ground. George and his brother Si — another native of Greece, who managed the Up-to-Date store — were so busy running three cafes that they had little time left to promote and finance athletics. As long as they lived, though, they followed sports events from baseball to hockey and track, the latter a favorite of the former Marathon runner.

The Idanha

The second field in which George Cordes was renowned was free dinners. Remembering the handout he got in Wyoming in bleak times, he opened his doors to everyone on one or more days of the traditional winter holidays — first with simple plates at the Up-to-Date and later with a complete spread from turkey and mashed potatoes to pumpkin pie at the Idanha. He did his best to see that no person in town needed to go hungry for lack of funds. At specified hours on the holidays he set aside a part of his dining rooms for the guests. He served them generously, asked no questions, and took no money. How many he helped is not known. The figure amounted to thousands. Cordes appreciated some publicity but was opposed to a glaring spotlight. He did not permit pictures during the dinners. He neither asked nor gave names of his guests. Everybody was welcome. Occasionally he had to decline payment from diners who did not realize it was a free meal. People who could afford turkey and trimmings did not know until they stepped to the silent cash register that the dinner was any different from the regular menu; it was not, except for the price.

An ad that appeared in *The Statesman* at Christmas

1933 is typical of the sentiment and philosophy of Cordes and the Idanha directors:

"It is logical that the Christmas day should be devoted to full enjoyment of the season's glorious holiday. What is more appropriate and pleasing than a delightful meal in a delightful restaurant? May we suggest the Idan-Ha cafe for a good old fashioned Christmas dinner?

"Cafeteria, 35 cents; table d'hote, 50 cents and 75 cents.

"Our annual free Christmas turkey dinner will be served today from 12 until 2:30 p.m. No cards needed. No questions asked. Everybody welcomed. Main dining room open to the public 3 p.m. Idanha Cafe and Cafeteria."

At the same season the Mechanafe was serving a special New Year dinner of six courses for fifty cents.

That season was also another occasion for Cordes to express his enthusiasm for basketball. When the Vandals came to Boise to play Boise Junior College he met with players and reminisced about old days. Stanton Hale, a former Vandal, was coach of the junior college in its first meeting with the university. Rich Fox, star of the championship teams in the 1920s, coached Idaho. Idaho won, 75 to 21. Howard Grenier, described as the "mammoth center" at six feet six, poured in a shower of points. Vernon Gilbert was tops for B.J.C. with seven. Once again Cordes treated the players, this time to coffee and cookies at the Up-to-Date. Such details are not in newspapers. Cordes related them years later when he was in mellow moods of recollection.

Free Christmas dinners for the needy continued more than thirty years. Crowds were largest during the Great Depression. Quantity and variety of the meals declined because of cost, but the same warm hospitality and nutrition were there.

The record crowd was about one thousand in 1937. Lots of people were broke, although New Deal programs were starting to stem the tide. During World War II attendance was moderate because there was more work on many fronts. The diners had tapered off to a few hundred by 1948.

Whenever asked whether he coordinated lists of his guests with the Salvation Army or public welfare agencies, Cordes said that was impossible because he had no names. Did he suspect there were some double diners? Perhaps there were, he said, but that was not his concern. He was pleasing himself by doing a charitable act. What he did in the Christian spirit of helping one's neighbor was nobody else's business.

All lines of activity were interrupted at the Up-to-Date in the spring of 1924 when the Strand Theatre burned. Along with it went the Up-to-Date and the Manitou Hotel. Damage was severe. The complex was restored. The fire was a double blow to George and Si Cordes. They had lived at the Manitou. Later, after he married, Si lived at the Bristol with his wife. Mr. and Mrs. George Cordes took a residence in the north end of Boise.

During World War II, Cordes had a hard time with the military. Health officials from Gowen Field inspected his premises regularly, as they did all eating establishments near the air base. They put the Idanha cafe on the black list because they found cracked dishes that could harbor germs. Cordes said he was doing the best he could. New dishes were expensive and hard to find. The restriction stood for several weeks, costing Cordes a chuck of money. He was able, though, to get a green light from the city health department, so he continued to serve civilians. Long before the war ended in the fall of 1945 the Idanha had a clean bill of health.

An unusual meal served in the back dining room at that period got a lot of notoriety. Thirty or so members of the Poacher's Club, a group of conservationists dedicated to sensible management of wildlife and to zany outbursts, undertook an experiment in bird eating. How about those four and twenty blackbirds baked in a pie? Those famous blackbirds of English history and rhyme? Somebody looked up the origin and figured the blackbirds must have been starlings. Great! Canyon County was up to its ears in starlings. There were flocks of thousands — some guessed millions — eating corn and wheat and everything else they could find on farms and feedlots. The tonnage they ate was a serious threat. Shooting was futile. Knock out a thousand, and ten thousand filled the gap. Poison removed more but was risky and distasteful.

The conservation group determined to do its bit by eating a batch. By setting the example and letting the news get around, the men thought, they might create a fad for starling. There were visions of starling à la Henry VIII, starling au gratin, starling mit noodles, starling on the half shell, starling under glass.

The appointed starling supplier, a knave with great marksmanship — proven by the fact that he could shoot the only merganser in a flock of mallards — took his trusty scattergun to a feedlot near Lake Lowell. With a target of more than five hundred starlings at fifteen yards he boomed both barrels. He killed sixty. Fifty-two were retrieved as fit for further treatment. Picking and cleaning fifty-two starlings is not a job for the average man. The gentleman in charge turned the chore over to his wife. By the time the task was done the kitchen was full of feathers and fighting words. The lady said it would be just fine with her if she never saw another starling. And, for that matter, men who shoot starlings and leave them to their wives.

Fifty-two plump little starlings, each about the size of a young robin, their rounded breasts standing in hillocks as large as thimbles, were delivered to the Idanha for roasting under the tender care of a man who said he had known all about starlings since he was a boy in Greece, where they were served with olives and just a nubbin of garlic.

At the appointed hour the pièce de resistance was unveiled. Roast starling with wild rice and brown bread began the repast. Ended it, too. Starling proved the most resistant pièce de resistance since Fighting Bob swallowed a golf ball. The nicest compliment of the day was that they tasted like erasers. Not many diners managed to get a taste. Starlings flew from under knives and forks, bounced along the table, jumped to the floor. The meal was not a total disaster — the rice and brown bread were delicious. Five starlings were ripped apart but not eaten. The other forty-seven, virtually the entire flock, ended in the Idanha garbage.

Cordes was embarrassed and apologetic. He said the starlings should have been baked in a pie, with plenty of liquid and long, slow cooking. The most optimistic of his diners thought three days would be about right. Cordes said he would cook the next batch that way. He guaranteed satisfaction. The men took him at his word. They did not try a second round. Starling à la Marathon was one of a kind.

Needless to say, the starling adventure was not recommended or tried for the free holiday dinners. Cordes was a man of compassion.

The Cordes brothers kept up their traditional treats many years after George left the Idanha. His lease was renewed a time or two, but he withdrew about the time the hotel was sold by the McMillan interests. The holiday meals were transferred back to the Up-to-Date, where they had begun in 1919. Silas Cordes died in 1963. George lived until the fall of 1971. A final free dinner for all comers was served as a sort of memorial on Christmas Day that year.

The IDAN-HA

Japan's surrender in 1945 created frantic days at the Idanha and all other hotels in Boise. Similar conditions existed elsewhere. Business was brisk. Rooms were at a premium. Military personnel coming home from far places, and being released from Gowen Field, jammed every cot for miles. When added to the tide of wives and families greeting their fighting men, the flood became critical. Men were permitted to sleep in the Idanha lobby. Four women on the way to join their husbands in another city found themselves stranded. Not only were there no rooms but there was no transportation by bus or train. They spent at least one night in the women's washroom at the railway depot.

Full houses were not an unmixed blessing. Because of exuberance or disregard of common decency, some customers hauled away blankets, pictures, pillows, and mirrors. Theft is not funny to proprietors. Whether GIs were responsible for the theft of Chief Idanha is not known. College boys are also blamed. The ceramic bust of an Indian with a feather in his hair was an ornament of the lobby for a long time. The Indian head was a trademark. Likenesses were glazed on Idanha china. Hardly a plate or cup remains. The big chief is long gone. A time or two he was swiped by revelers and returned. To guard against another theft, old Idanha was wired so that his eyes glowed red when the bust was moved. Somebody got him, eyes and all.

Hope that he might have gone to Portland proved false. The Hoyt Hotel there, putting on historic airs, advertised that some of its bar fixtures were from the Idanha. Boise people who examined them said it was true, but the collection did not include the chief. The treasures are no longer there — the Hoyt has closed.

When it comes to misadventures involving the birds and the beasts, Hotel Boise must get the nod for two of its contenders. Top billing goes to the grand champion steer of the Western Idaho District Fair. The fat and frisky Hereford, weighing nearly half a ton, was displayed in a log corral in the lobby because the management had bought him for a pretty price at the auction of 4-H stock. His quarters in the large lobby, where there was a cheery fireplace, were piled with straw. He had plenty of water and whatever rations were most appropriate for a beast of purple-ribbon quality.

The steer was a drawing card. Guests swarmed in to admire and to pat. Only one fly disturbed the ointment. The animal, named Virgil by some citizens because Virgil McGee, hotel manager, engineered the deal, was not friendly to city people. He liked ranchers with hay in their hair and the smell of barns. Metropolitan types, who said sweet nothings while offering popcorn balls and candied apples, gave him a pain. On the second night of his weekend he went over the hill. He broke through a corner of the pen, took a look at the dining room, backed off, and made a beeline for Eighth Street, through glass doors that fortunately opened outward. He was almost to the Federal Building when a stockman drove him into an alley. The steer was cornered behind a garbage bin, and a stock truck hauled him to the butcher.

On another occasion at the Boise, a swarm of bees was knocked loose on the mezzanine during a convention. They stung a number of legislators in the elevator and the coffee shop before buzzing off.

Both the Bristol and the Owyhee were unexpected hosts to frightened pheasants. The birds came to town during hunting season. One crashed into an office window at the Owyhee. Another, on a separate date, took refuge in an auto parked in front of the Bristol. When the driver came out the bird gave him a scare.

It was not birds or beasts that stirred up excitement at the Idanha about fifteen years ago. An entertainer at a night club had a room there. She was a belly dancer, snake charmer, and whatnot.

She developed a platoon of admirers. One of her devoted fans found out where she lived. He asked for a date. She declined. In the small hours one night, after she had finished her turns at the club, he knocked on her door. She opened it a few inches but did not invite the guy in. She had no need to. He was halfway down the hall yelling like a stabbed Indian. Behind him wriggled an eight-foot python. The serpent was part of her act — also her bodyguard. The racket roused so many guests the place was bedlam. Within a few minutes the dancer collared her snake and locked it in a closet. As far as hotel personnel can remember, the suitor did not call again.

Another Idanha adventure into the animal world had to do with reindeer. Grady Carothers, a Texan in the Dasher and Prancer business, stopped in Boise with eleven head on a September day in 1953. He said several of the reindeer, picked up in Alaska, had been attacked by bear or wolves on the Alcan Highway and needed a veterinarian. While he put up at the hotel, he left his patients with Dr. William Ewing. The veterinarian and his wife, Marjorie, several years a city council member, recall the occasion. Mrs. Ewing remembers that their yard was full of reindeer while Dr. Ewing attended to the wounds. Neighbors wondered if they were about to launch an early Christmas.

There was also the matter of a cougar killed with a rock near Middleton. The fight did not take place at the Idanha but was related there by a guest. The story goes that Charles Bannister and Indian Jake were attacked by a hungry mountain lion on a bank of Indian Creek, a tributary of Boise River. The lion leaped on Indian Jake. Bannister hit the cougar with a rock, breaking its hold on Jake. The blow also damaged the lion's shoulder. Jake jumped up and fractured the cougar's skull with a rock. Bannister and Jake suffered only scratches. They measured the dead lion at nine feet and a bit. It is seldom that any cougar ever killed is less than nine feet.

Much earlier, in 1911 to be precise, a mountain man from Elk City brought two fearsome dogs to town. He was not allowed to keep them at the Idanha. His purpose was to show that his dogs could catch and kill coyotes. He said they were part coyote and part husky. He had been breeding them for five generations, until he had what he believed was the right mixture of speed, cunning, and savagery. He said they had killed all the coyotes in his area, and he was ready to tackle Ada and Canyon counties. How his efforts came out is not known, except that coyotes still live in those precincts. One, in fact, was so bold during the time the Elk City exterminator was on the prowl that it invaded the Meridian city limits and bit a man digging a ditch. The ditch digger did not wait for a killer dog. He clobbered the coyote with his shovel.

None of the husky-coyotes would have made a snack for White Rover, an Alaskan wolfhound in residence at Hotel Boise in April 1932. He weighed nearly two hundred pounds and stood six feet six on his hind legs, a yard high on all four pads. He also appeared at a department store and the children's home.

The IDAN-HA

The big fire was September 9, 1951. For the Idanha it was a near miss. For the Sonna Building it was curtains. The fire broke out on a Sunday morning. How it started is not known. Max Maxwell, Idanha elevator operator, turned in the alarm and started evacuating guests when Mrs. Myrtle McCormick, a maid, told him she smelled smoke. Within seconds there was lots of smoke. It billowed from the second floor of the Sonna Building. Maxwell and the maid pounded on doors. The message was: "Get your pocketbook and run. Use the stairs. Leave the elevator for firemen."

Guests grabbed a few clothes and hit for the lobby. They were soon joined by Ansgar Johnson and some other tenants of the Sonna Building. Johnson, a veteran photographer, was unable to reach his studio because of smoke. At least seven other business and professional offices on the second floor were filled with smoke. Fingers of flame darted along the hall. There were two explosions about an hour apart. An insurance office, an advertising agency, and other businesses were heavily damaged. The J. C. Penney store and the Newberry store on the first floor were almost total losses. Arthur Tetrick, a spokesman for the Broadbent

Estate, owner of the building, estimated the loss at a million or more.

Charles Brock, a fireman, was hurt when he stepped into a hole in the floor. Eleanor Stull, a teacher who lived at the Idanha, and Argo Cantrell, who lived at the Bluebird Hotel and was spending the night with a gentleman friend, were overcome by smoke. They recovered.

Mrs. Ansgar Johnson, manager of the Idanha, said a sprinkler system saved the hotel, She said it had been installed four years earlier, after a hotel fire in Atlanta, Georgia. The water that saved the Idanha from flame created a mess in the hotel. It flowed from floor to floor until there was more than an inch in the cafe. Cordes and his staff saved as much food as they could and sopped up the deluge when firemen gave the all clear.

Ansgar Johnson set up a temporary studio in the Idanha with equipment he salvaged. Most of his negatives, considered priceless because of the scenes and people they depicted through many years, were destroyed.

Confidence that the Idanha would survive was exemplified by a man who came in off the street while smoke billowed and asked for a room. He was advised to join the evacuated crowd until the situation cleared. He came back later and was given a room. All the rooms had to be aired. Not until they were redone did they lose the smell of barbecued carpet.

Mrs. Johnson had been manager of the hotel a relatively short time before the fire. She took charge in the final years of her father's life. Thomas McMillan died in 1952 at the age of eighty-eight. Mrs. Johnson operated the Idanha until June 1962, when she sold to the Broadbent Estate.

John Broadbent was born in England in 1835. He came to Boise by way of California, like so many pioneers who had sunk their picks in goldfields before they settled down to more stable activities. His first try was a jewelry store. A publication called "The Story of a Builder," says he had an ambition to become Idaho's wealthiest citizen. He went a long way toward that goal before he died in 1922 at the age of eighty-seven. With the jewel shop as the nestegg he expanded to real estate in the business heart of Boise and in residential developments. He owned or had a major interest in numerous buildings. Year after year he was in the upper echelon of commercial and home construction as was W. E. Pierce, a builder who put up and managed many structures in the city. Pierce was also a guiding spirit in the electric railway that looped the valley and was the creator of Pierce Park, a resort that became the Plantation Golf Club.

Broadbent lived and died a bachelor. The estate was divided among twelve nephews and nieces. Arthur Tetrick, a great-grandnephew, came to Boise in 1949 to manage the estate. His wife, Alice, soon assumed a major role. Peppy and perky, she pumped her enthusiasm into the business and into civic and social causes. When Tetrick died in 1969 and she became president of the Broadbent Foundation she continued his policies of faith in the future of Boise's core. She qualified her position by saying: "Many of the downtown buildings were put up in haste by early settlers. These are not worth saving. But there are others, very well constructed, which should be preserved."

Among those that have been preserved is the Idanha. It wasn't easy. There were times when it seemed certain the hotel would become rubble. Individuals and organizations concerned about saving meaningful landmarks succeeded in having the hotel placed on the National Register of Historic Places in 1976, the Bicentennial Year. Jess Jennison was Idanha manager at the time. Alice Tetrick, now Mrs. John Bellomo of San Francisco, credits Jennison with much of the hotel's success during the Broadbent period.

Alice Tetrick was born in a small Alaskan town where her father was a lawyer. She attended a one-room school with a pot-bellied stove. She graduated from the University of Washington and went to work for United Airlines in San Francisco as a reservation clerk. She nearly got the ax when the supervisor found out she was reading schedules backward. She was in Arthur Terick's office being fired when the national headquarters phoned that she had won an award for the highest sales that month. She kept her job.

In Boise she put her talents to work in such things as the Red Cross, March of Dimes, and St. Luke's Hospital. In the midst of all that and work for the Broadbent Foundation, she helped manage a Little League baseball team on which her son, Reed, played.

She was a driving spirit at the Idanha. "I do not know my title on the books," she said, "but I called myself vice president of moving furniture."

Many changes in decor were made. Policies were revamped, too.

"Jess Jennison was hired as manager in 1963," Mrs. Bellomo said, "and continued in that position under the new owners until he reached retirement age. The Idanha became his life, and he performed a magnificent job. He provided the cash flow our company needed pending purchase by the Boise Redevelopment Agency of other downtown Boise properties that we couldn't afford to bring up to modern standards under the threat of condemnation."

Former and new managements found good news and bad news in an article in a national news magazine regarding the problems of redevelopment. The good news was that Boise was recognized as a city of about one hundred thousand trying to improve its business heart. The bad news was the reference to the Idanha as a once-elegant hotel that had become a sort of flophouse and was now being restored to respectability. Mrs. Roxie Johnson was ready to wring that writer's neck. If he had shown up she might have pointed out some of the splendid rooms still tastefully maintained by the hotel's new regime — before she hurled him from the bay window of the Clarence Darrow suite.

False reports of the Idanha's death revived memories of the real end, in the 1930s, of the Capitol Hotel Building on the south side of Main between Eighth and Ninth. The hotel had been as full of history in its youth as it was of cobwebs at the end. The Capitol was built before 1900, making it older than the Idanha. In the beginning it spread over a wide chunk of street front and had many rooms. Time took heavy toll. It ceased to exist as a hotel in 1928. Some rooms were rented to transients. By 1940 the vicinity was the site of a Woolworth store, with a paint store next door. The whole thing bit the dust when redevelopment cleared several blocks for the new Jerusalem which has yet to show its shiny portals.

The Capitol's main claim to fame was the belief that Owen Wister wrote at least some chapters of *The Virginian* there. At the time the weary bones of the building were ripped apart there news stories and orations redolent of cowboys, schoolmarms, and rustlers. One editorial writer was so impressed by the fact that a boardwalk and a board fence were put up in front of the Capitol site while it was being dismembered, that he conjured up pictures of Trampas and the Virginian stalking each other behind the barricades. The duel was dramatically portrayed. One could almost see Gary Cooper pull his revolver, shoot Trampas, and say "Yup," when the schoolmarm asked if the villain was dead.

Opportunities have existed, and still do, for flights of rich imagery regarding events at the Idanha.

If all the bellhops, elevator operators, and taxi drivers associated with the Idanha held out their hands at one time, it would take the Bank of America to dish out the tip. More legend than fact surrounds these minor characters, although there is no doubt about the identity of some.

Lobby gossip has it that a son of Tommy Manville, the marrying man, hopped bells and ran the elevator while his mother, the wife de jour, was in residence to get a quickie Idaho divorce. The story is that he wanted something to do. He was a nice kid, so the hotel let him serve the customers. Because Idanha records have been lost or burned there is little to follow in sniffing out the truth.

The young bellhop remains anonymous who embarrassed William Jennings Bryan when the Great Commoner was in his underwear expecting a tub of ice and suddenly was confronting a female reporter as well as the ice.

Max Maxwell gained notice because he was the elevator operator who turned in the alarm when the Idanha was threatened by the Sonna Building fire in 1951.

From the beginning in 1901 the elevator, a marvel of the era, was run by an operator who turned a crank, slammed doors, and tried to stop the carriage within reasonable stepping distance at each floor. One of the bonuses was a colorful jacket and a cap. The elevator was remodeled several times. Uniforms for operators also changed. Toward the end of the era there were no uniforms. Finally the elevator succumbed to do-it-yourself. That's the way it is in 1983. It glides up and down as quietly as a spider on a curtain. It has its hangups between floors, as all elevators do. It usually obeys the push button. But it isn't as interesting as the human beings who used to shift the gears and give tongue to all the gossip worth hearing, mingled with baseball scores and election returns.

An elevator operator who had previously worked in the mines gave a load of gentlemen a scare one day. Karl Bonham, recently retired as vice president of Syms-York, says it happened about forty years ago, when he was working for the printing company as salesman and public relations representative. During a convention of county assessors at the Idanha he boarded the elevator with a group he was taking to dinner. Bonham sang out, "Cut the rope," a term familiar to everybody in the Coeur d'Alene mining district where he had lived as a boy. The operator had been a lift man in the mines, and when he heard the order he let the cage drop like a shot. It hit the shock absorbers in the basement and bounced back up a floor or two. The elevator operator said that it had been reflex action and that he wouldn't do it again. Bonham says he doesn't know whether he did or not, but he suspects that several of his assessor friends used the stairs thereafter.

Joseph C. Grannon, eighty-five, a longtime Idanha resident and former elevator man, was murdered in April 1975

This photograph of an unidentified young man hangs in the lobby. It has been called "Uncle of the Unknown Soldier."

near the elevator he had run many years before. He was shotgunned by John Peter Nelson, a transient, presumably deranged. Grannon was walking down the hall, carrying a jug of water and leaning on a cane, when Nelson stepped out of his room and without warning shot him in the chest. Nelson then shot himself to death. Coroner Steve Jablonski and Ada County Attorney Dave LeRoy investigated but failed to find a cause for the shooting. There may have been a dispute. One woman said she heard noises but didn't know what they were. Nearly everyone was watching television, and the consensus of those residents was that the gunfire was on the tube. The official finding was murder and suicide.

The late Victor McLeod, a Hollywood writer, started his career shining shoes at the Idanha. He spoke of those days when he visited Boise in 1945, his first trip to the old hometown in nearly thirty years. He was born in Nampa and moved to Boise as a baby. His father was John McLeod, a barber. Victor polished shoes in his dad's shop and elsewhere as his business expanded. One of his special customers was Jim Kelly, the restaurant man. In those times Jim would have his shoes shined in the street while he rested himself and his pushcart. McLeod, a cousin of Mrs. Fred Taylor and Don McLeod of Boise, wrote scripts for

Bob Burns, Bing Crosby, and Edgar Bergen. Just before he came to Boise he had been on a trip to Alaska with one or two of his stars who were entertaining servicemen.

A bellhop whose record is vivid but whose name is John Doe Elusive, is said to have made a pot of money in Alaska. He came back and tried to buy the Idanha. No dice. No foundation for the story, either, in contemporary reports. Could be true, but it sounds fantastic.

Quite factual was a taxi driver who met all trains for the Idanha before the Main Line was built. He was involved in the arrest of a baggage car. Federal agents filed suit against the car, jerked it out of the train, and cited it in court for harboring alcoholic beverages. The taxi driver was mixed up in the case because he allegedly picked up booze from the naughty car and hauled it somewhere — not the Idanha, of course. He was released. The baggage car was forgiven, too.

The IDAN-HA

Whatever "Idanha" means in Indian tongue or fantasy, it was a popular name for firms. In addition to the hotel, restaurants, and some others already mentioned, there were at various times the following:

Idanha Pool Hall, 924 Main, George and Christ Karras, proprietors (they also had a shoeshine parlor); Idanha Optical Company, a few doors from the hotel; Idanha Natural Mineral Water Company, 708 West Idaho, a branch of the Capitol Liquor Company, E. A. Eieger, manager; the Idanha Auto Livery, George R. German, Jr., manager; The Idanha Taxi, successor to the livery, William Atherton, proprietor; Idanha Shoe Shine, operated by the Karras men (moved to Grove Street under the name of Idaho Shoe Shine Parlor); and the Idanha Buffet, 924 Main, a bar owned by David Neumann and others.

Many hotels have existed in Boise during the career of the Idanha. About forty-five years ago a man in the business counted nearly eighty hotels, rooming houses, boarding-houses, and similar accommodations. Although some took only one or two guests infrequently, they qualified as public facilities. A partial list includes:

Pacific Hotel, 203 North Ninth, managed in the 1920s

by Albert W. Beck of Mayfield, an in-law of the Obediah Corder family and therefore related to the McMillans who ran the Idanha. Albert Beck was the father of James O. Beck, one-time director of the Idaho Fish and Game Department.

Hotel Grand, 1025 Main, where Frank Blackinger was proprietor in 1925 and later. Blackinger had been manager of the Capitol in the 900 block on Main in earlier years.

The Overland, successor in name to the Overland of pioneer times, 213 South Ninth.

The Central, successor in name to another famous inn, Ninth and Grove, noted because the weekly rate was $2.

DeLamar House on Grove, built by Capt. J. R. DeLamar and operated as a rooming house, a home for deaf and blind children, a swanky men's club, and, its last years before the wrecking ball, a boardinghouse.

The Sherman House on North Seventh, which was split and moved to two new locations for residences and apartments.

The New Overland, Eleventh and Main, constructed before the Owyhee, E. B. Miller, manager. When the New Overland quit, the other Overland namesake came into being.

One of the larger hotels attracted many guests to Tenth and Grove. In the beginning it was the Bristol. This "new and modern" hotel was built in 1919 by J. A. Yates and was operated by Dr. H. A. Gaglegly. Later it was owned by H. D. Cosho. Mrs. Maude Cosho, legislator and prime mover in many city and state activities, became manager at his death. A son, John Cosho, was a clerk and assistant manager. The Bristol was sold in 1939 to the Milner Hotel Company, a coast-to-coast chain. It then became the Milner, with Courtney Rider as manager. The Milner fell to the wrecking ball in 1965. That was the finish of a building that had many mellow memories. It was greatly appreciated for its long lobby on Grove Street. Comfortable chairs and sofas were an admirable vantage point for watching pedes-

Johnson and Son

The Bristol Hotel, about 1934. This hotel, also called the Milner during part of its career, was a contemporary of the Idanha many years. It was torn down to make room for Boise's redevelopment.

trian traffic. If anything was doing in that corner of town, people in the Milner lobby quickly found out about it.

The Owyhee, Eleventh and Main, and Hotel Boise, Eighth and Bannock, have already been discussed.

Passengers arriving by rail were a mainstay of hotel business before autos proved they were here to stay. From its beginning, the Idanha met all trains at the Front Street Station. First it had horse-drawn carriages. Then it switched to cars. Trips to and from the passenger depot were short and didn't cost much. For a time they were free for guests arriving at the hotel. As recently as the 1930s, when there was a longer trip from the depot on the bench, the taxi fare could be charged to your Idanha room.

Train traffic continued to be important to innkeepers long after the advent of the automobile. For one thing, people who had engagements in a certain city could not rely on cars, which were likely to develop engine trouble, flat tires, or broken axles. For security and dependability there was nothing like the train. It might be a little late, but it would get there. You wouldn't be way out in the desert huddled over a sagebrush fire waiting for a new wheel or a gas tank to replace one that had dropped into a badger hole. So hotels paid attention when locomotives whistled. The sound meant bread and butter.

Boise was not on the main line. The railroad bypassed the city. A branch, known as "the stub" served Boise from Kuna. For many years Idaho's largest city seethed under the slight. Campaigns for a spot on the main line finally succeeded in 1925. During the drive for funds the Idanha pledged a hefty sum. The contribution was approved at a meeting of hotel directors, who said they joined in the community effort although the new station far from the heart of town was likely to hurt hotel business. There was apprehension that new hotels would spring up closer to the station and grab the trade. Worry over changes in travel patterns, for better or worse, did not at that time include the mushrooming of motels, which proved a far greater blow to the traditional hotel than the decline of railways or the relocation of passenger stations.

The main line arrived April 16, 1925. A forty-year dream was realized. Carl R. Gray, president of the Union Pacific, was man of the hour. Thirteen bands, numerous floats, and lots of horses appeared in one of Boise's most elaborate parades. Gov. C. C. Moore and Mayor E. B. Sherman escorted the railroad executive.

Nearly all the pictures used by *The Statesman* in a special edition were by Johnson and Son, a matter of gratification to the Idanha because Ansgar Johnson was the husband of the proprietor's daughter.

For the trivia file, the first train was on time. The second was twenty minutes late. Gagsters had fun with the first train. Governor Moore lost his ticket. The conductor was persuaded to let him stay aboard by paying a fine.

A few days after the first train reached Boise on the

main line, a story in the morning paper said that a Pullman passenger lifted his window shade and peered into the dark. "What town is this, porter?" he asked. "Not been named yet, sir," said the porter. "Way off down there someplace is Boise."

How the new station affected business at the Idanha and other hotels is hard to determine. Other factors were having an influence. The entire business of serving the traveling public was in the mixmaster.

The day the main line came, the Idanha looked bravely to the future in a quarter page ad: "Proud successor to the Overland," it said. "Construction of the Idanha marked the commencement of Boise's permanent building activities. Scene of notable historic banquets. Plenty of bathrooms. A real home for travelers. A Mecca for Idaho people. Every accommodation for tourists. Headquarters for Idaho stockmen from the beginning. Excellent cafeteria and cafe. Low rates for such splendid service."

The mention of tourists was a sign that a new age was starting. Hotels had to realize that thousands of families were loading their jalopies with kids, tents, boxes of grub, and tire patches for trips to fabulous spots. In Boise the fad had special meaning. The city had one of the first — if not the first — municipal tourist parks in the nation. For a nightly rate of about fifty cents, motorists were welcome to pitch their tents while they enjoyed a swim at the Nat or shopped downtown. The site is now Municipal Park. In its budding years the Boise Kiwanis Club manned the registration booth. On one occasion the club sold all space in the park, finally renting the ticket booth to a couple of travelers.

Popularity of the tourist park opened a rift between hotels and newspapers. Gushes of publicity about the tourist park drew complaints from hotels. They said, in effect, "How about us? We've been here all the time, your friend, neighbor, and advertiser. Cool this tourist stuff." Newspapers replied that the park was newsworthy. Hotels dropped their ads, and in retaliation the papers stopped running the daily list of hotel arrivals. The tempest was soon over, and tourism, hotel ads, and guest lists continued on their amiable courses.

The IDAN-HA

A romance that was nurtured at the Idanha ended in homicide at Cascade. Valley County people favored the Idanha. Perhaps because pioneers in stock raising and lumber production had stayed at McMillan's hotel, younger generations stayed there. Weekend groups of half a dozen were often there, having fun and bringing news of such sled-dog racers from their vicinity as Smoky Stover and Thula Ghelan, famous for winning at such places as Ashton, Idaho, and Truckee, California.

Among the Long Valley people attending an Idanha weekend in the 1930s were George Stonebraker of Cascade and Thelma Harp. Friendship that began in McCall advanced when they met again with mutual friends at the Idanha, and romance ripened into marriage. Evidence at a district court trial in Cascade in 1945 shows the marriage was not a happy one. Thelma shot George at their ranch home near Cascade in the presence of several dinner guests. He died on the spot. A witness said George had called Thelma vile names. She burst into tears and went to her room. Soon "the attractive brunette," as a newswriter identified her, "returned with a gun and shot George twice." Later she said, "Why did I kill him when I love him so much? I hope I hang for it." She didn't.

Mrs. Stonebraker was defended by George Donart and Fred Taylor. Thomas Feeney prosecuted. Judge A. O. Sutton presided.

Temporary insanity was the primary argument presented by the defense. Testimony suggested that George had threatened Thelma several times, once with a pitchfork. Two doctors said she had temporary amnesia on the night of the shooting.

A secondary defense, not offered by attorneys but highlighted by the press, was the beauty of Mrs. Stonebraker. Time after time reporters referred to her as attractive, comely, and shapely. The jury deliberated less than two hours and found her not guilty. The late Andy Anderson, a logging contractor, jumped up at the verdict and yelled, "Hooray!" Judge Sutton admonished him to be quiet. Anderson left the courtroom. He stuck his head in the window and shouted another "hooray."

The press still appeared more excited about the defendant's apearance than her freedom. "Mrs. Stonebraker, 31, has dark brown hair which she brushes until it glistens," a story said. "She is of medium build with a shapely figure and comely legs."

Two noted visitors, in the multitude of important characters who visited the Idanha, had special influence on the hotel's reputation. One was Will Rogers, the other was Sally Rand. They had little in common except perhaps Rogers' famous saying: "I never met a man I didn't like."

Rogers was in Boise in March 1927. He gave his lariat and laugh show at the Pinney for an audience in stitches from start to finish. He was the only person in the performance. His sole prop was a chair he lifted from the orchestra pit. He chewed gum, spun his rope, and reeled off witty bits for a couple of ours. Although he did not stay at the Idanha, he gets credit for spreading the name throughout the country. Boise friends took him on a tour of the town. He noted the towers of the Idanha and remarked on the architecture as he proceeded to the Nat and the baseball park on Warm Springs Avenue. Noting the ceme-

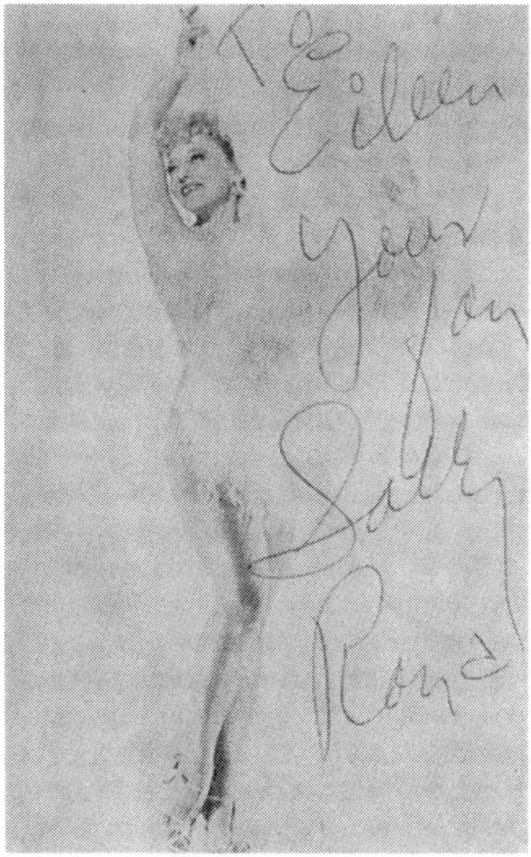

Sally Rand, the fan dancer, autographed many photos like this during an engagement in Boise in her later years. She stayed at the Idanha.

tery across the street from the ball grounds he said he guessed that was where they left the umpires. During a reception at the home of Calvin Cobb, *Statesman* publisher, he asked again about the turreted hotel. And about the other one a block away.

"The laughing hotels," he said. "The Idanha-ha and the Owyhee-hee."

From time to time the quip is credited to others. It may be that Rogers did not say it first. At any rate, he usually gets the credit. The idea enhances the histories of both hotels.

Rogers played polo during his Boise visit. He proved to players and followers that he could ride and score as well as he rattled off funny stories. He twitted Mayor Eagleson for chuckholes in Boise streets. He said they were not safe even to fly over. Criticized himself because he had said Pocatello was bigger than Boise, he said he must have counted boxcars.

Did he read fiction? "Some," he said. "The newspapers."

On the prophetic side he forecast another war: Germany against the world. "They won't *shoot* at you," he said. "They will drop things on you. You will have to go up in the air or dig in. And we are the only country in the world that uses the air solely for oratory."

Boise felt a keen sense of loss when Rogers was killed in an airplane accident in Alaska in 1935. There was no merriment at the laughing hotels.

Sally Rand, the fan-dancing sensation of the Chicago fair, spent a week at the Idanha in 1973. She said she was delighted with the atmosphere — a mixture of modern comfort and old fixtures such as brass bedsteads, bathtubs on iron feet, pull cords for electric lights. The idea that she found a feather bed is without foundation. At that time, indeed, Sally was no longer flinging her feathery fans as she did in Chicago. She was in Boise for an engagement at a night spot. She was nearing her seventieth birthday. Still possessing nice legs and a charming personality, she concentrated on stories of her career interspersed with advice. She made a particular hit by visiting old soldiers at the Veterans Hospital. During appearances before service clubs she said a good word for the younger generation. She said she was teaching a Sunday school class in her California hometown to keep the young people from going to the dogs.

In an interview with a *Statesman* reporter Sally said:

"Everyone knows blue programs have been going on since Greek times, but I never thought anyone would brag about it, like the actresses in some of these films."

No woman's libber, she said: "I love being a girl and a sex symbol. It's what women were made for."

She said this about shoes:

"A woman's feet should always look as beautiful as the rest of her. Thick heels don't do a thing for me." (She wore size 4½ shoes with spike heels.)

"Pink does wonders for blondes. Every girl, especially blondes, should have a pink dress."

Members of the Idanha staff remember Sally Rand as a delightful lady. She was friendly, kind, and almost reserved in manner while off the stage. She autographed pictures for several hotel people. Most were such treasures they were stolen. Few of the many pictures she distributed during the week are to be found.

The Idanha was an important launching pad for state legislation for several decades. As the residence of Goveror Gooding, it was a center of policy-making almost from its beginning, and it continued that role for many legislative sessions. Political bigwigs began to switch to the Owyhee when it was constructed, and it soon became Republican headquarters. When Hotel Boise was opened in 1930 it was considered the Democratic stronghold. The Idanha was in the middle. It regarded both parties as acceptable customers. Because the Idanha had only a small dining room, it was not a suitable place for the political galas that became annual showcases for candidates and their platforms.

Many legislators of different political faiths stayed at the Idanha. Among the memorable was C. B. ("Caribou") Wilson, a Democratic representative from Caribou County. It was often said that he was the founder or inventor of Caribou County. He was not. The county, created in 1919, was named for Caribou Fairchild, an early prospector. But Caribou Wilson did not go out of his way to deny the honor.

Jolly, bearded, and deep voiced, Representative Wilson met his obligations in the house of representatives with an attitude appreciated by his constituents back home and applauded by his associates in Idaho's parliament. When there was something on the agenda that needed his attention he gave it. When the business had no bearing on Soda Springs, he leaned back and read his newspaper. At least he read it for a few minutes. Then he slept — or apparently slept. It was hard to tell when he was hidden behind the newspaper and the thicket of whiskers that cascaded down to his belt. He roused for roll calls. Almost invariably he voted no. When he said no it could be heard in Meridian. Wilson said he usually voted no because the law books already had too many acts. He believed in streamlined government.

Jokers hid an alarm clock in his desk. It went off in the middle of a dreary afternoon. Caribou shot up in his chair and shouted, "No." When the house calmed and the speaker advised Representative Whiskers that no roll call was in progress, the gentleman from Caribou sank back into his nap.

At night, Caribou was bright-eyed and bushy-tailed. None of the daytime sluggishness remained. He enjoyed big meals and lively conversation in happy company. People who liked to party found him a charming guest. He told stories of his youth and his recent life in Alexander, a hamlet near Soda Springs. He also told stories that Chaucer and Balzac could have added to their collections.

He was a considerate gentleman. Friends who escorted him to the Idanha, where he lived during several sessions, remember that he made a ritual of looking at his watch. If it was past 10 o'clock, which it was by several hours, he would say it was a little late and he must be quiet. He would then take off his shoes and tiptoe across the lobby and up the stairs, not using the elevator because the noise might bother somebody. Joe R. Wilson, managing editor of *The Statesman* during some of the years Caribou was in the legislature, recalls early morning breakfasts with the representative after nights of spirited conversation. He said Caribou's favorite snack at that hour was finnan haddie and a boiled potato.

Another legislator, George R. Jones of Owyhee County, who served several terms in the house, stayed at the Idanha. He was later a member of the public utilities commission. In retirement he lived at the Idanha. He took pleasure in getting the hotel's mail every morning from the post office. The Idanha was honored to have a former legislator and utilities commissioner as its letter boy.

A story goes that construction of the west and final wing of the statehouse in 1919 was made possible by a compromise at the Idanha. The chairman of a major committee concerned with public buildings was staying at the Idanha. To be sociable he invited various legislators to his room from time to time to have a cup of tea. Prohibition was in effect, and officers of the law felt he was not serving tea. They confiscated a jug from the legislator's closet. They said it was a good grade of Owyhee moonshine. There were intimations that an arrest was likely.

"Suit yourselves," said the sociable solon. He said it to members of the legislature eager to pass the appropriation for the statehouse. "I happen to have the bill in a safe place. I can keep it until you ice skate with the devil. I just might do that unless you see that the legal papers about possession of liquor disappear. And one thing more. It would be nice if somebody brought back the jug."

Lo and behold, the papers disappeared. It was all a mistake. The statehouse bill came out and sailed through. The story usually ends with a statement that Owyhee moonshine showed up in a certain closet at the Idanha. Not one jug but two.

Ansgar Johnson was a great man to meet for a morning cup of coffee. Along about 10 o'clock, if he didn't have to take a passport photo or have an assignment to shoot scenery with a backdrop of fleecy clouds he was generally to be found in the Idanha Cafe. Friends sought him out. They considered themselves fortunate to hear him talk Scandanavian with Greek Cordes or mystify giggling waitresses with his compliments. He was also a source of news. In a casual way, without presuming to know anything that was not already in the public domain, he dropped hints about events that became front-page news. Ansgar was admired for his affection and consideration for his father, Jons Peter, originator of the photography firm. He often interrupted his work to attend to a request from "Pop."

Mr. and Mrs. Johnson had three sons. Peter is chief executive of the Bonneville Power Administration. Mack is a New York businessman. Ansgar, Jr., is a Boise photographer. Ansgar, Sr., died in November 1981. Mrs. Johnson lives in Boise, occasionally visiting the Idanha to see how things are going.

Ansgar, Sr., took few pictures of the Idanha. Nearly all that he did shoot were lost in the Sonna Building fire. A picture that he didn't take, and one that he and other cameramen wish they had, was of a group of Indians at the Idanha. About twenty Bannocks and Shoshoni from Fort Hall were brought to Boise for the centennial of Old Fort Boise in 1934. They set up tents in Julia Davis Park, where they displayed beadwork and demonstrated tribal dances.

As night approached, their advisor, a white man from Blackfoot, said they should be getting ready to bed down. They said not in tents in the park. No, they said they would stay downtown in the hotel with the Indian chief as its symbol. They won. They spent the night at the Idanha and ate breakfast in the cafe. No smoky tents for those proud visitors.

Several native red men had a look through the Idanha lobby when Buffalo Bill Cody was in Boise much earlier with his Wild West Show. Buffalo Bill himself, accompanied by Iron Tail, chatted with friends in easy chairs. A special friend Buffalo Bill met there was Bishop James B. Funsten. Cody and Funsten were mutual admirers from Wyoming days. Cody strolled to the bishop's house for an evening cigar and had the bishop as a guest at the wild west performance.

Bishop Funsten, incidentally, was a patron of the Idanha. He leased entire floors for clergy conferences.

The IDAN-HA

A question often put to hotel people is: "What is the best kind of clientelle?" It depends on the place and the historic time. For the Idanha, categories were broad, of course, at that time and since. There is agreement in the trade that good customers are those who pay their bills and act like ladies and gentlemen.

Laws about public lodging being what they are, collecting money from cheaters is not a bowl of cherries. Allowing for ramifications and refinements in the jungle of legalese, there is an understanding that a registered guest is not subject to eviction for nonpayment as long as he has personal property in the room. Sometimes that personal property is a battered suitcase containing a toothbrush and a dirty shirt. The host has measures, however, to protect his interest. He may not confiscate the luggage of a suspected fraud, but he can prevent entrance to the room until financial adjustments are made. There are sections of the code that offer more satisfaction to the innkeeper than chicanery. Even so, as Jess Jennison quotes a Salt Lake hotel manager: "It isn't the skips that skip that cost you money. It's the skips that stay."

During his years managing the Idanha for the Broadbent

interests, Jennison said some of the finest clientelle were Canadians. They liked the Idanha because it reminded them of Canadian and British hotels.

Another class of excellent customers, he said, were truck drivers. Contrary to opinion in some quarters that truckers are a grubby, rough lot, Jennison found them fine men. They were disciplined, he said. Many were college boys away from home to make cash. After they washed up, the truck drivers looked and acted like respectable businessmen. The Idanha was a little leery about accepting them on a group basis, but once the decision was made it was applauded. Drivers occupied rooms in shifts. Twenty-five or thirty took rooms for eight hours. Others came in as they completed their runs. Rooms were cleaned and beds made up for the second platoon. The truckers behaved themselves, paid promptly, and were liked by other guests.

At the other end of the scale, inductees were a headache. On their final fling as civilians they spent their energies tearing up things and stealing towels.

More than towels have been taken. A spokesman for the Idanha says that in recent years there is a compulsion for people to throw things out of hotel windows. Paper airplanes are common. The spokesman said something came flying out of a room and nearly hit him as he was standing in the street. It was a book of burning matches. Many times transients have tossed ice cubes, one by one, on passing pedestrians. They also steal fire extinguishers. One that was hurled out of a window was spotted on a nearby roof where it cannot be reached.

The morning after a couple of youths checked out it was discovered they had torn down the wall between the bedroom and living room of the suite. There was a heap of rubble on the floor. Nobody in adjoining rooms heard any noise.

Limousines have become part of the Idanha trademark. The most luxurious taxi was a Rolls-Royce, obtained about twelve years ago to take guests to the airport. Sad to say, the $35,000 vehicle broke down a few weeks after it went to

An elegant Rolls-Royce was the pride of the Idanha's taxi service. Josephine DuMaurier, chauffeur, kept it gleaming.

work. It has not been repaired. For one thing, parts are hard to get. Josephine Jones DuMaurier was the chauffeur. She later became operating manager of the hotel.

The next limousine was a 1948 Packard of generous proportions. It rests most of the time at the curb. Its license plate, "IDANHA," draws attention to the hotel, but the venerable Packard seldom has passengers. It is available for hire with liveried chauffeur. Built for endurance and speed as required, the old sedan rolled out for an historical parade in 1982 but had to drop out because creeping at fifteen

Senator Woody Nelson, goodwill ambassador with flashes of P. T. Barnum, is public relations man at the Idanha. He got a dozen votes for U.S. President in 1980.

miles per hour heated the engine nearly to the breaking point.

Something else distinctive the Idanha has going for it is Woody Nelson, known as Senator Woody. He is ambassador of goodwill and tourism. Combining the genes of P. T. Barnum and a rotund politician — and now and then sprouting a Colonel Sanders goatee — Senator Woody is the modern epitome of the old-fashioned greeter. From a background in journalism and radio he served for a time as public relations consultant to Robert E. Smylie, former Idaho governor. Jumping on the stump himself, he started at the top. In 1980 Senator Woody was a candidate for president of the United States. He got votes, too. About a dozen. He did not concede to Ronald Reagan until the polls closed in California. He blames his defeat in part on the fact that he did not start soon enough. The campaign got off the ground about Halloween.

The year of 1980 was not a total loss, though. In August the senator was named employee of the month by unanimous vote of Idanha employees. At that time he had spent seven years on the staff, had become Senior Statesman among his colleagues, and for six years had been a resident of what he was pleased to call the "Grand Old Lady of Main Street." He had been night auditor, trainer of clerks, security guard, and desk clerk. He welcomed many distinguished guests. He took pleasure and pride in telling one and all the glories of the Idanha, not omitting to suggest present comforts and future charm.

One of his accomplishments is the Idanha Song. Here it is:

O beautiful for spacious rooms
For king-size beds galore,
For suites so clean, a limousine,
And there's a whole lot more.
O Idanha, the Idanha
For hospitality
We'll be your guide;
Just come inside
And see what you can see.

O beautiful for eighty years
And more, since nineteen-one,
For relaxation without fears,
For sleep when day is done.
O Idanha, the Idanha
Your home away from home;
Here's where to stay,
Your hideaway,
Wherever you may roam.

O beautiful for turret rooms
With old and new decor,
They're all good news
With wondrous views;
And there's a whole lot more.
O Idanha, the Idanha
The landmark old hotel
You'll appreciate,
You'll say it's great,
We'll really treat you swell.

Senator Woody and the venerable Packard are familiar symbols of the Idanha

The IDAN-HA

Every hotel has its unusual moments. Here are a few from the Idanha ledger:

An engineer lived in a second-story apartment. A woman told the clerk she saw a shotgun in his window. Police investigated. The engineer had a citizen's band radio in his car in the parking lot across the street. He was afraid somebody would rip it off, so he rigged up a dummy holding a shotgun, placed it in his window, and kept the lamp on all night.

Three teenagers were drinking beer on the sixth floor when they discarded a carton of empties out the window. Twenty-four empties crashed onto the street, narrowly missing a couple of taxi drivers. When the night manager threw the drinkers out, they complained to police that the manager was cruel man because it was 2 A.M. and starting to rain.

A dazzling brunette took a room one night. Six months later she checked in again. The night clerk noticed she used a different name.

"I have never been in this hotel before," she said.

The clerk said she was very much like a lady who had been there. "I think I must have a twin sister," she said, "because other people have told me the same thing. I have always suspected I was adopted."

As she walked to the elevator the clerk realized that she and her predecessor were both wearing the same black dresses, black stockings, black shoes, and pearl necklaces. A comparison of registration cards showed identical writing. The street address in Pocatello was the same.

Why the charade was carried on nobody ever learned.

There is an unseen ghost on one floor. Curtains flap when there is no breeze. Doors mysteriously open and shut. Things go bump in the night. Locks come unlocked. Moans sound from the elevator shaft. A "presence," like the ghost of Hamlet's father, stalks past doorways.

An interesting woman stayed one night about 1973. She called the desk to report that little men from outer space were attacking her. The night man went to the rescue. He could not open the door until the little old lady moved the large pieces of furniture she had placed as a barricade. Assured that the little green men were not shooting darts at her, she retired to an apparent peaceful sleep and did not remember the attack next morning.

Late one rainy evening a girl carried her bicycle into the lobby and started riding around, knocking down chairs and threatening destruction to the entire premises. When assisted in prompt departure she protested that she had a right to ride in a public place. She crashed on the front steps. Amid threats to sue she picked up the pieces and was never heard from again.

A couple of seedy-looking characters staggered to chairs in the lobby and went to sleep. Because of their snores and the smell of sour wine, the night clerk asked police to remove them. A neatly dressed gentleman nearby assisted. The clerk thanked him, being particularly grateful because he feared the gentleman had been disturbed by the drunks. Police arrived. Before they took care of the bums they said hello to the nice gentleman.

"Glad to see you, Jim. Better come along, too. Been wondering where you were."

It turned out the gentleman was a con artist wanted for several stings.

Then there was the sweet young thing who was escorted to a room in which the heat had not been turned on. She called in a few minutes to say it wasn't warm yet. The desk clerk said everything would be fine shortly. To be even more friendly and efficient, he rang the room an hour later.

"Comfy?" he asked, when a woman answered. "Anything more we can do to make your stay pleasant?"

"Yes," came the reply. "You can explain why you are calling us."

"Isn't this 410?" asked the clerk.

"No it isn't. This is 510 and my husband and I are annoyed."

After that, said the clerk, he made sure he plugged in the right room.

Many years after the Sonna Building fire of 1951, weekend celebrators tampered with a sprinkler head. The system burst into numerous showers. Damage was in the thousands of dollars. The men who caused it disappeared.

A classic wheeze of hotels everywhere has not escaped the Idanha:

"Call me at 6, please," asked a guest.

"All our 6 o'clock calls are booked," said the clerk.

"Then call me twice at 3 o'clock," said the guest.

The IDAN-HA

The cocktail lounge in the Idanha basement has been through many changes. At the outset, or thereabouts, it was Weeds-a-Go-Go, named by a little girl who remarked to Alice Tetrick Bellomo that there were weeds down there. During the 1970s it was: Rileys, operated by Riley Johnson; the Coffee Pot, leased by several; the Slammer, leased by Ralph Palmeri; G.J.'s Lounge, run by three men; and the Landmark Lounge, operated by Cecil Lee and later by John Vickers, who was also manager of the Idanha. After a time as a storage cellar, the club was in line for revival in the winter of 1983 as something else.

Peter Schott's Continental Restaurant took over and remodeled the Idanha Coffee Shop in the 1970s. The restaurant offers cuisine that brings back memories of the elegant repasts of Charles Grout. Prices, however, are somewhat different. Schott was formerly executive chef at Sun Valley. The menu is long on Austrian dishes. Schott has another reataurant in the Saratoga Hotel at Caldwell.

The Idanha barbershop in the basement has become a hair-styling emporium. Little boys no longer have the thrill of a haircut in that memorable chamber. When the barber said, "And I suppose, son, you will also be wanting a shave?" the world was one's oyster.

A tailoring shop next to the barbershop succumbed to fire. A newsstand above the basement quarters, occupying a corner of the lobby, was knocked out in the summer of 1982 by a terrific wind. Plate glass was smashed.

The hotel itself was owned in 1983 by Idanha Properties. Calvin Jensen is partner-manager. White-Savage is a part of the parent company. New alignment was being considered late in 1983.

In point of longevity, the hotel honors these people:

Helen Collord was an employee forty-eight years. Betty Medlin was a desk clerk for twenty-six. Mrs. Chloa Irwin is the senior resident. She has lived at the Idanha thirty years. "I liked it when I first came, and I still find it a splendid place," she says. "It has everything I want. The people are very thoughful." Before her retirement, Mrs. Irwin was a saleslady at Brookover's.

A roster of notable characters who have played a part in the history of the Idanha would fill a book. In addition to such people as Ethel Barrymore, Harry Orchard, Clarence Darrow, Walter Johnson, William Jennings Bryan, and Sally Rand, whose visits have been related, the list includes:

Jim Corbett, world champion heavyweight fighter, toured the country on behalf of good sportsmanship and clean living. He appeared at the Pinney Theatre and is believed to have skipped rope in the Idanha lobby as an added attraction.

Little Jim Corbett, a scalawag who tried to cash in on the name, was revealed as a fraud and allegedly jumped off a Boise bridge. His body was not found. The sheriff said it was a fake suicide.

Margaux Hemingway, model and actress, who visited the lounge, asked Senator Woody if he were an American Indian. He said he was not but would be proud to be one.

Presidents Theodore Roosevelt, William Howard Taft, and Benjamin Harrison visited the hotel on quick tours of the city.

Anna Maria Alberghetti, Peg Bracken, Ruth Buzzi, Clint Eastwood, Diane Keaton, Gordon MacRae, Joan Mondale (wife of the former vice president), Gordon Munford, Beverly Sassoon, Abigail Van Buren, Lawrence Ferlinghetti (poet), Ted Lewis, Gifford Pinchot, Scatman Crothers, Ernestine Schumann-Heink, and Pablo Casals. They are not listed in chronological order, obviously. Some were not born when others were famous.

While name dropping, how about Jimmy Stewart? He dropped in for coffee when he was stationed at Gowen Field.

Steve Brodie, the bartender of bridge-jumping fame, brought his vaudeville act to Boise. The show did not amuse the press. The Bowery Boys were termed coarse and disappointing. Brodie gained notoriety for jumping off Brooklyn Bridge in 1886 to win a $200 bet. He survived the drop of 135 feet but was arrested for attempting suicide. A classic story of the episode says that the father of Jim Corbett, the fight champ, went to Brodie's saloon to congratulate the jumper.

"Did you really do it?" Corbett asked.

"Sure I jumped off the bridge."

"Off it! Any damn fool can jump off it. I thought you jumped over it."

Brodie would have been a natural for the Idanha. For a time it seemed he could be traced to that inn. Alas, he was in Boise in 1896, before the Idanha was built. In the realm of fantasy there is the picture of Brodie jumping from the famous verandah to a streetcar.

In all parts of the state there are couples who remember the Idanha as the place they spent their honeymoon. Many return for anniversaries.

A celebrity corner for portraits of noted guests is being planned.

Phil Batt, former lieutenant governor, often plays clarinet at jam sessions in the Continental Room. Gov. John Evans sometimes dines in the restaurant. Nearly all Idaho governors since 1901 have stayed or attended meetings at the Idanha. Patronage may have doubled after the Owyhee changed from its original style as a full-fledged hotel and

Hotel Boise became the Hoff Building — for offices, shops, and cafes, but with no hotel rooms. The end of the Republican-Democratic hotel rivalry could have left clear sailing for the Idanha if the motel age had not arrived. Genuine, traditional hotels are scarce. The Idanha is one that survives because, as its management says, it combines the atmosphere and warmth of the past with modern adjustment to a changing society.

If there are ghosts in the Idanha they may be the spirits of Steunenberg, Barrymore, Madame Nordica, Lord Fingall, and Walter Johnson whispering about the glories of their era and advising their successors in a muddled world to be of good cheer. Things will get better, even though we cannot expect a corner suite for two dollars or an Idanha Christmas dinner for a dollar, including cigars for the men and candy for the ladies. As in the beginning, the Idanha spirit bubbles.

Printed in the United States
77232LV00004B/202-267